Endpoint Protection Platform Market Complete Self-Assessment Guide

The guidance in this Self-Assessment is based on Endpoint Protection Platform Market best practices and standards in business process architecture, design and quality management. The guidance is also based on the professional judgment of the individual collaborators listed in the Acknowledgments.

Notice of rights

You are licensed to use the Self-Assessment contents in your presentations and materials for internal use and customers without asking us - we are here to help.

Trademarks

Table of Contents

3

About The Art of Service

The Art of Service, Business Process Architects since 2000, is dedicated to helping stakeholders achieve excellence.

Defining, designing, creating, and implementing a process to solve a stakeholders challenge or meet an objective is the most valuable role… In EVERY group, company, organization and department.

Unless you're talking a one-time, single-use project, there should be a process. Whether that process is managed and implemented by humans, AI, or a combination of the two, it needs to be designed by someone with a complex enough perspective to ask the right questions.

Someone capable of asking the right questions and step back and say, 'What are we really trying to accomplish here? And is there a different way to look at it?'

With The Art of Service's Standard Requirements Self-Assessments, we empower people who can do just that — whether their title is marketer, entrepreneur, manager, salesperson, consultant, Business Process Manager, executive assistant, IT Manager, CIO etc... —they are the people who rule the future. They are people who watch the process as it happens, and ask the right questions to make the process work better.

Contact us when you need any support with this Self-Assessment and any help with templates, blue-prints and examples of standard documents you might need:

http://theartofservice.com
service@theartofservice.com

Included Resources - how to access

Included with your purchase of the book is the Endpoint

Protection Platform Market Self-Assessment Spreadsheet Dashboard which contains all questions and Self-Assessment areas and auto-generates insights, graphs, and project RACI planning - all with examples to get you started right away.

How? Simply send an email to
access@theartofservice.com
with this books' title in the subject to get the Endpoint Protection Platform Market Self Assessment Tool right away.

You will receive the following contents with New and Updated specific criteria:

• The latest quick edition of the book in PDF

• The latest complete edition of the book in PDF, which criteria correspond to the criteria in...

• The Self-Assessment Excel Dashboard, and...

• Example pre-filled Self-Assessment Excel Dashboard to get familiar with results generation

• In-depth specific Checklists covering the topic

• Project management checklists and templates to assist with implementation

Purpose of this Self-Assessment

This Self-Assessment has been developed to improve understanding of the requirements and elements of Endpoint Protection Platform Market, based on best practices and standards in business process architecture, design and quality management.

It is designed to allow for a rapid Self-Assessment to determine how closely existing management practices and procedures correspond to the elements of the Self-Assessment.

The criteria of requirements and elements of Endpoint Protection Platform Market have been rephrased in the format of a Self-Assessment questionnaire, with a seven-criterion scoring system, as explained in this document.

In this format, even with limited background knowledge of Endpoint Protection Platform Market, a manager can quickly review existing operations to determine how they measure up to the standards. This in turn can serve as the starting point of a 'gap analysis' to identify management tools or system elements that might usefully be implemented in the organization to help improve overall performance.

How to use the Self-Assessment

On the following pages are a series of questions to identify to what extent your Endpoint Protection Platform Market initiative is complete in comparison to the requirements set in standards.

To facilitate answering the questions, there is a space in front of each question to enter a score on a scale of '1' to '5'.

1 Strongly Disagree

2 Disagree

3 Neutral

4 Agree

5 Strongly Agree

Read the question and rate it with the following in front of mind:

**'In my belief,
the answer to this question is clearly defined'.**

There are two ways in which you can choose to interpret this statement;
1. how aware are you that the answer to the question is clearly defined
2. for more in-depth analysis you can choose to gather evidence and confirm the answer to the question. This obviously will take more time, most Self-Assessment users opt for the first way to interpret the question and dig deeper later on based on the outcome of the overall Self-Assessment.

A score of '1' would mean that the answer is not clear at all, where a '5' would mean the answer is crystal clear and defined. Leave emtpy when the question is not applicable or you don't want to answer it, you can skip it without affecting your score. Write your score in the space provided.

After you have responded to all the appropriate statements in each section, compute your average score for that section, using the formula provided, and round to the nearest tenth. Then transfer to the corresponding spoke in the Endpoint Protection Platform Market Scorecard on the second next page of the Self-Assessment.

Your completed Endpoint Protection Platform Market Scorecard will give you a clear presentation of which Endpoint Protection Platform Market areas need attention.

Endpoint Protection Platform Market Scorecard Example

Example of how the finalized Scorecard can look like:

Endpoint Protection Platform Market Scorecard

Your Scores:

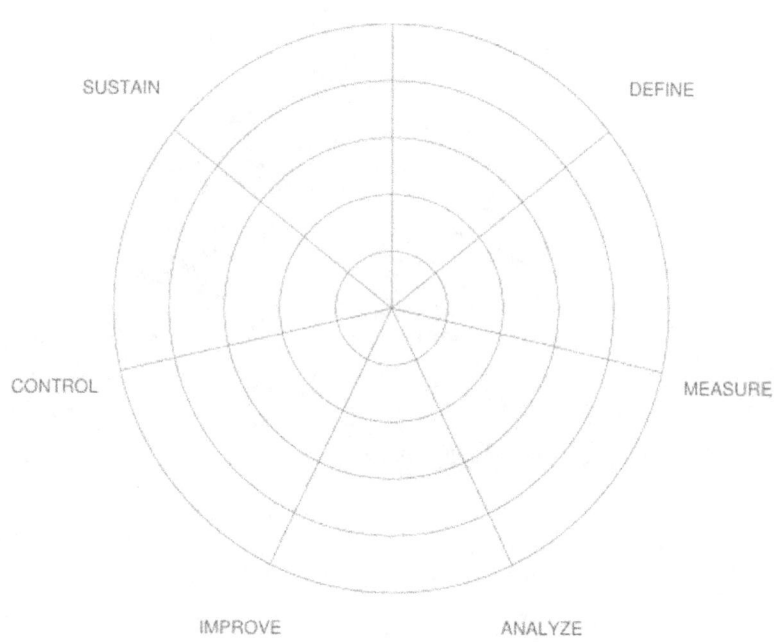

BEGINNING OF THE SELF-ASSESSMENT:

CRITERION #1: RECOGNIZE

INTENT: Be aware of the need for change. Recognize that there is an unfavorable variation, problem or symptom.

In my belief, the answer to this question is clearly defined:

5 Strongly Agree

4 Agree

3 Neutral

2 Disagree

1 Strongly Disagree

1. What do you need to start doing?
<--- Score

2. Think about the people you identified for your endpoint protection platform market project and the project responsibilities you would assign to them, what kind of training do you think they would need to perform these responsibilities effectively?

<--- Score

3. Will a response program recognize when a crisis occurs and provide some level of response?
<--- Score

4. What tools and technologies are needed for a custom endpoint protection platform market project?
<--- Score

5. What does endpoint protection platform market success mean to the stakeholders?
<--- Score

6. What do employees need in the short term?
<--- Score

7. Consider your own endpoint protection platform market project, what types of organizational problems do you think might be causing or affecting your problem, based on the work done so far?
<--- Score

8. Are your goals realistic? Do you need to redefine your problem? Perhaps the problem has changed or maybe you have reached your goal and need to set a new one?
<--- Score

9. How do you assess your endpoint protection platform market workforce capability and capacity needs, including skills, competencies, and staffing levels?
<--- Score

10. What is the extent or complexity of the endpoint

protection platform market problem?
<--- Score

11. To what extent does each concerned units management team recognize endpoint protection platform market as an effective investment?
<--- Score

12. What endpoint protection platform market coordination do you need?
<--- Score

13. What endpoint protection platform market capabilities do you need?
<--- Score

14. What would happen if endpoint protection platform market weren't done?
<--- Score

15. What is the problem and/or vulnerability?
<--- Score

16. What are the clients issues and concerns?
<--- Score

17. Are employees recognized for desired behaviors?
<--- Score

18. Are employees recognized or rewarded for performance that demonstrates the highest levels of integrity?
<--- Score

19. Who needs to know about endpoint protection

platform market?

<--- Score

20. What needs to be done?

<--- Score

21. Will it solve real problems?

<--- Score

22. What are the minority interests and what amount of minority interests can be recognized?

<--- Score

23. What is the smallest subset of the problem you can usefully solve?

<--- Score

24. Are controls defined to recognize and contain problems?

<--- Score

25. Is it needed?

<--- Score

26. Are you dealing with any of the same issues today as yesterday? What can you do about this?

<--- Score

27. What training and capacity building actions are needed to implement proposed reforms?

<--- Score

28. Is the need for organizational change recognized?

<--- Score

29. Looking at each person individually – does every

one have the qualities which are needed to work in this group?
<--- Score

30. Are there any specific expectations or concerns about the endpoint protection platform market team, endpoint protection platform market itself?
<--- Score

31. Why the need?
<--- Score

32. Which issues are too important to ignore?
<--- Score

33. Is the quality assurance team identified?
<--- Score

34. What is the problem or issue?
<--- Score

35. When a endpoint protection platform market manager recognizes a problem, what options are available?
<--- Score

36. Which needs are not included or involved?
<--- Score

37. Which information does the endpoint protection platform market business case need to include?
<--- Score

38. What problems are you facing and how do you consider endpoint protection platform market will circumvent those obstacles?

<--- Score

39. How do you recognize an objection?
<--- Score

40. What endpoint protection platform market problem should be solved?
<--- Score

41. Who needs what information?
<--- Score

42. Does the problem have ethical dimensions?
<--- Score

43. Are there recognized endpoint protection platform market problems?
<--- Score

44. How do you recognize an endpoint protection platform market objection?
<--- Score

45. What is the recognized need?
<--- Score

46. What situation(s) led to this endpoint protection platform market Self Assessment?
<--- Score

47. Who should resolve the endpoint protection platform market issues?
<--- Score

48. Did you miss any major endpoint protection platform market issues?

<--- Score

49. How are you going to measure success?
<--- Score

50. Do you need different information or graphics?
<--- Score

51. Who needs budgets?
<--- Score

52. How are the endpoint protection platform market's objectives aligned to the group's overall stakeholder strategy?
<--- Score

53. How do you identify subcontractor relationships?
<--- Score

54. What vendors make products that address the endpoint protection platform market needs?
<--- Score

55. Do you know what you need to know about endpoint protection platform market?
<--- Score

56. Does endpoint protection platform market create potential expectations in other areas that need to be recognized and considered?
<--- Score

57. Are there endpoint protection platform market problems defined?
<--- Score

58. What activities does the governance board need to consider?

<--- Score

59. Will endpoint protection platform market deliverables need to be tested and, if so, by whom?

<--- Score

60. What are the stakeholder objectives to be achieved with endpoint protection platform market?

<--- Score

61. How many trainings, in total, are needed?

<--- Score

62. Will new equipment/products be required to facilitate endpoint protection platform market delivery, for example is new software needed?

<--- Score

63. Where is training needed?

<--- Score

64. Who needs to know?

<--- Score

65. Are losses recognized in a timely manner?

<--- Score

66. Are there any revenue recognition issues?

<--- Score

67. What are the expected benefits of endpoint protection platform market to the stakeholder?

<--- Score

68. To what extent would your organization benefit from being recognized as a award recipient?
<--- Score

69. Why is this needed?
<--- Score

70. Are problem definition and motivation clearly presented?
<--- Score

71. What information do users need?
<--- Score

72. As a sponsor, customer or management, how important is it to meet goals, objectives?
<--- Score

73. Does your organization need more endpoint protection platform market education?
<--- Score

74. How are training requirements identified?
<--- Score

75. What endpoint protection platform market events should you attend?
<--- Score

76. Are there regulatory / compliance issues?
<--- Score

77. What else needs to be measured?
<--- Score

78. What are your needs in relation to endpoint

protection platform market skills, labor, equipment, and markets?
<--- Score

79. Have you identified your endpoint protection platform market key performance indicators?
<--- Score

80. How can auditing be a preventative security measure?
<--- Score

81. How do you take a forward-looking perspective in identifying endpoint protection platform market research related to market response and models?
<--- Score

82. Do you need to avoid or amend any endpoint protection platform market activities?
<--- Score

83. Can management personnel recognize the monetary benefit of endpoint protection platform market?
<--- Score

84. Where do you need to exercise leadership?
<--- Score

85. What creative shifts do you need to take?
<--- Score

86. What are the endpoint protection platform market resources needed?
<--- Score

87. How does it fit into your organizational needs and tasks?
<--- Score

88. What prevents you from making the changes you know will make you a more effective endpoint protection platform market leader?
<--- Score

89. Do you recognize endpoint protection platform market achievements?
<--- Score

90. How much are sponsors, customers, partners, stakeholders involved in endpoint protection platform market? In other words, what are the risks, if endpoint protection platform market does not deliver successfully?
<--- Score

91. What are the timeframes required to resolve each of the issues/problems?
<--- Score

92. Whom do you really need or want to serve?
<--- Score

93. Do you have/need 24-hour access to key personnel?
<--- Score

94. Who else hopes to benefit from it?
<--- Score

95. What needs to stay?
<--- Score

96. How do you identify the kinds of information that you will need?
<--- Score

97. What should be considered when identifying available resources, constraints, and deadlines?
<--- Score

Add up total points for this section:
_ _ _ _ _ = Total points for this section

Divided by: _ _ _ _ _ _ (number of statements answered) = _ _ _ _ _ _
Average score for this section

Transfer your score to the endpoint protection platform market Index at the beginning of the Self-Assessment.

CRITERION #2: DEFINE:

INTENT: Formulate the stakeholder
problem. Define the problem, needs and
objectives.

In my belief, the answer to this
question is clearly defined:

5 Strongly Agree

4 Agree

3 Neutral

2 Disagree

1 Strongly Disagree

1. What are the requirements for audit information?
<--- Score

2. What defines best in class?
<--- Score

3. Is there a completed, verified, and validated high-level 'as is' (not 'should be' or 'could be') stakeholder process map?

<--- Score

4. Does the scope remain the same?
<--- Score

5. What information should you gather?
<--- Score

6. Is there a completed SIPOC representation, describing the Suppliers, Inputs, Process, Outputs, and Customers?
<--- Score

7. What happens if endpoint protection platform market's scope changes?
<--- Score

8. What key stakeholder process output measure(s) does endpoint protection platform market leverage and how?
<--- Score

9. Will a endpoint protection platform market production readiness review be required?
<--- Score

10. Scope of sensitive information?
<--- Score

11. Are resources adequate for the scope?
<--- Score

12. Is the scope of endpoint protection platform market defined?
<--- Score

13. What is the scope?
<--- Score

14. Is scope creep really all bad news?
<--- Score

15. Is there a endpoint protection platform market management charter, including stakeholder case, problem and goal statements, scope, milestones, roles and responsibilities, communication plan?
<--- Score

16. Is the current 'as is' process being followed? If not, what are the discrepancies?
<--- Score

17. What scope to assess?
<--- Score

18. What knowledge or experience is required?
<--- Score

19. What is the definition of success?
<--- Score

20. Who is gathering endpoint protection platform market information?
<--- Score

21. Is the improvement team aware of the different versions of a process: what they think it is vs. what it actually is vs. what it should be vs. what it could be?
<--- Score

22. How did the endpoint protection platform market manager receive input to the development of a

endpoint protection platform market improvement plan and the estimated completion dates/times of each activity?
<--- Score

23. Are task requirements clearly defined?
<--- Score

24. In what way can you redefine the criteria of choice clients have in your category in your favor?
<--- Score

25. What sources do you use to gather information for a endpoint protection platform market study?
<--- Score

26. Have all of the relationships been defined properly?
<--- Score

27. What critical content must be communicated – who, what, when, where, and how?
<--- Score

28. How does the endpoint protection platform market manager ensure against scope creep?
<--- Score

29. Is there any additional endpoint protection platform market definition of success?
<--- Score

30. How was the 'as is' process map developed, reviewed, verified and validated?
<--- Score

31. Is the endpoint protection platform market scope complete and appropriately sized?
<--- Score

32. Has the endpoint protection platform market work been fairly and/or equitably divided and delegated among team members who are qualified and capable to perform the work? Has everyone contributed?
<--- Score

33. What is in the scope and what is not in scope?
<--- Score

34. Who defines (or who defined) the rules and roles?
<--- Score

35. How do you manage unclear endpoint protection platform market requirements?
<--- Score

36. When is the estimated completion date?
<--- Score

37. Who is gathering information?
<--- Score

38. Why are you doing endpoint protection platform market and what is the scope?
<--- Score

39. What specifically is the problem? Where does it occur? When does it occur? What is its extent?
<--- Score

40. What system do you use for gathering endpoint

protection platform market information?
<--- Score

41. How do you hand over endpoint protection platform market context?
<--- Score

42. Do the problem and goal statements meet the SMART criteria (specific, measurable, attainable, relevant, and time-bound)?
<--- Score

43. How often are the team meetings?
<--- Score

44. Has the improvement team collected the 'voice of the customer' (obtained feedback – qualitative and quantitative)?
<--- Score

45. Is there a critical path to deliver endpoint protection platform market results?
<--- Score

46. Are roles and responsibilities formally defined?
<--- Score

47. How do you build the right business case?
<--- Score

48. What are the tasks and definitions?
<--- Score

49. Does the team have regular meetings?
<--- Score

50. Has the direction changed at all during the course of endpoint protection platform market? If so, when did it change and why?
<--- Score

51. What information do you gather?
<--- Score

52. Have all basic functions of endpoint protection platform market been defined?
<--- Score

53. Has a high-level 'as is' process map been completed, verified and validated?
<--- Score

54. What are the endpoint protection platform market use cases?
<--- Score

55. How is the team tracking and documenting its work?
<--- Score

56. How do you keep key subject matter experts in the loop?
<--- Score

57. What are the compelling stakeholder reasons for embarking on endpoint protection platform market?
<--- Score

58. Do you have organizational privacy requirements?
<--- Score

59. Are all requirements met?

<--- Score

60. The political context: who holds power?
<--- Score

61. Have the customer needs been translated into specific, measurable requirements? How?
<--- Score

62. Has your scope been defined?
<--- Score

63. Who are the endpoint protection platform market improvement team members, including Management Leads and Coaches?
<--- Score

64. Is the work to date meeting requirements?
<--- Score

65. What are the record-keeping requirements of endpoint protection platform market activities?
<--- Score

66. Is there regularly 100% attendance at the team meetings? If not, have appointed substitutes attended to preserve cross-functionality and full representation?
<--- Score

67. Has/have the customer(s) been identified?
<--- Score

68. Who approved the endpoint protection platform market scope?
<--- Score

69. Will team members regularly document their endpoint protection platform market work?
<--- Score

70. What constraints exist that might impact the team?
<--- Score

71. What are the dynamics of the communication plan?
<--- Score

72. Where can you gather more information?
<--- Score

73. What are the core elements of the endpoint protection platform market business case?
<--- Score

74. Is the team equipped with available and reliable resources?
<--- Score

75. What are the rough order estimates on cost savings/opportunities that endpoint protection platform market brings?
<--- Score

76. Is endpoint protection platform market currently on schedule according to the plan?
<--- Score

77. Are there any constraints known that bear on the ability to perform endpoint protection platform market work? How is the team addressing them?

<--- Score

78. Will team members perform endpoint protection platform market work when assigned and in a timely fashion?
<--- Score

79. How will variation in the actual durations of each activity be dealt with to ensure that the expected endpoint protection platform market results are met?
<--- Score

80. What endpoint protection platform market services do you require?
<--- Score

81. How do you gather the stories?
<--- Score

82. Are the endpoint protection platform market requirements complete?
<--- Score

83. Has a endpoint protection platform market requirement not been met?
<--- Score

84. Do you all define endpoint protection platform market in the same way?
<--- Score

85. If substitutes have been appointed, have they been briefed on the endpoint protection platform market goals and received regular communications as to the progress to date?
<--- Score

86. What are the Roles and Responsibilities for each team member and its leadership? Where is this documented?
<--- Score

87. What sort of initial information to gather?
<--- Score

88. Has anyone else (internal or external to the group) attempted to solve this problem or a similar one before? If so, what knowledge can be leveraged from these previous efforts?
<--- Score

89. How are consistent endpoint protection platform market definitions important?
<--- Score

90. Have specific policy objectives been defined?
<--- Score

91. What is out of scope?
<--- Score

92. What baselines are required to be defined and managed?
<--- Score

93. What was the context?
<--- Score

94. Has a project plan, Gantt chart, or similar been developed/completed?
<--- Score

95. What is the definition of endpoint protection platform market excellence?
<--- Score

96. Is the team adequately staffed with the desired cross-functionality? If not, what additional resources are available to the team?
<--- Score

97. How do you manage scope?
<--- Score

98. How do you catch endpoint protection platform market definition inconsistencies?
<--- Score

99. Are customer(s) identified and segmented according to their different needs and requirements?
<--- Score

100. How and when will the baselines be defined?
<--- Score

101. Is data collected and displayed to better understand customer(s) critical needs and requirements.
<--- Score

102. Is full participation by members in regularly held team meetings guaranteed?
<--- Score

103. How would you define endpoint protection platform market leadership?
<--- Score

104. What would be the goal or target for a endpoint protection platform market's improvement team?
<--- Score

105. What is in scope?
<--- Score

106. What intelligence can you gather?
<--- Score

107. Are different versions of process maps needed to account for the different types of inputs?
<--- Score

108. Has everyone on the team, including the team leaders, been properly trained?
<--- Score

109. What customer feedback methods were used to solicit their input?
<--- Score

110. When is/was the endpoint protection platform market start date?
<--- Score

111. How will the endpoint protection platform market team and the group measure complete success of endpoint protection platform market?
<--- Score

112. How do you think the partners involved in endpoint protection platform market would have defined success?
<--- Score

113. What are (control) requirements for endpoint protection platform market Information?
<--- Score

114. What is a worst-case scenario for losses?
<--- Score

115. What is out-of-scope initially?
<--- Score

116. Is endpoint protection platform market required?
<--- Score

117. What is the scope of the endpoint protection platform market effort?
<--- Score

118. Has a team charter been developed and communicated?
<--- Score

119. Are the endpoint protection platform market requirements testable?
<--- Score

120. What gets examined?
<--- Score

121. What are the boundaries of the scope? What is in bounds and what is not? What is the start point? What is the stop point?
<--- Score

122. Is endpoint protection platform market linked to key stakeholder goals and objectives?
<--- Score

123. How have you defined all endpoint protection platform market requirements first?
<--- Score

124. Are accountability and ownership for endpoint protection platform market clearly defined?
<--- Score

125. When are meeting minutes sent out? Who is on the distribution list?
<--- Score

126. Are required metrics defined, what are they?
<--- Score

127. What are the endpoint protection platform market tasks and definitions?
<--- Score

128. Is special endpoint protection platform market user knowledge required?
<--- Score

129. Is the endpoint protection platform market scope manageable?
<--- Score

130. What is the scope of endpoint protection platform market?
<--- Score

131. What is the context?
<--- Score

132. Are there different segments of customers?

<--- Score

133. How do you gather requirements?
<--- Score

134. What is the worst case scenario?
<--- Score

135. What scope do you want your strategy to cover?
<--- Score

136. How do you manage changes in endpoint protection platform market requirements?
<--- Score

137. Is there a clear endpoint protection platform market case definition?
<--- Score

138. Is it clearly defined in and to your organization what you do?
<--- Score

Add up total points for this section:
_ _ _ _ _ = Total points for this section

Divided by: _ _ _ _ _ _ (number of statements answered) = _ _ _ _ _ _
Average score for this section

Transfer your score to the endpoint protection platform market Index at the beginning of the Self-Assessment.

CRITERION #3: MEASURE:

INTENT: Gather the correct data. Measure the current performance and evolution of the situation.

In my belief, the answer to this question is clearly defined:

5 Strongly Agree

4 Agree

3 Neutral

2 Disagree

1 Strongly Disagree

1. Have you included everything in your endpoint protection platform market cost models?
<--- Score

2. What could cause delays in the schedule?
<--- Score

3. Has a cost center been established?
<--- Score

4. What could cause you to change course?
<--- Score

5. How much does it cost?
<--- Score

6. What are the estimated costs of proposed changes?
<--- Score

7. How do you verify performance?
<--- Score

8. What causes extra work or rework?
<--- Score

9. What disadvantage does this cause for the user?
<--- Score

10. What would it cost to replace your technology?
<--- Score

11. How do you verify endpoint protection platform market completeness and accuracy?
<--- Score

12. When should you bother with diagrams?
<--- Score

13. Are there any easy-to-implement alternatives to endpoint protection platform market? Sometimes other solutions are available that do not require the cost implications of a full-blown project?
<--- Score

14. What drives O&M cost?

<--- Score

15. What details are required of the endpoint protection platform market cost structure?
<--- Score

16. What are the uncertainties surrounding estimates of impact?
<--- Score

17. Why do you expend time and effort to implement measurement, for whom?
<--- Score

18. How is performance measured?
<--- Score

19. Are the units of measure consistent?
<--- Score

20. How will your organization measure success?
<--- Score

21. When a disaster occurs, who gets priority?
<--- Score

22. How can you manage cost down?
<--- Score

23. What are the costs?
<--- Score

24. How do you verify and develop ideas and innovations?
<--- Score

25. What are the costs of delaying endpoint protection platform market action?
<--- Score

26. Who is involved in verifying compliance?
<--- Score

27. What are the operational costs after endpoint protection platform market deployment?
<--- Score

28. What is measured? Why?
<--- Score

29. What are the endpoint protection platform market key cost drivers?
<--- Score

30. When are costs are incurred?
<--- Score

31. What does a Test Case verify?
<--- Score

32. What happens if cost savings do not materialize?
<--- Score

33. How long to keep data and how to manage retention costs?
<--- Score

34. How do you measure lifecycle phases?
<--- Score

35. How do you measure efficient delivery of endpoint protection platform market services?

<--- Score

36. Where is the cost?
<--- Score

37. How do you verify and validate the endpoint protection platform market data?
<--- Score

38. How are measurements made?
<--- Score

39. Are there measurements based on task performance?
<--- Score

40. Is the cost worth the endpoint protection platform market effort ?
<--- Score

41. What can be used to verify compliance?
<--- Score

42. How do you measure success?
<--- Score

43. How can you measure the performance?
<--- Score

44. What causes mismanagement?
<--- Score

45. Are you taking your company in the direction of better and revenue or cheaper and cost?
<--- Score

46. How do you measure variability?
<--- Score

47. Do you effectively measure and reward individual and team performance?
<--- Score

48. What tests verify requirements?
<--- Score

49. What is the cost of rework?
<--- Score

50. Which measures and indicators matter?
<--- Score

51. What are the costs and benefits?
<--- Score

52. What are the costs of reform?
<--- Score

53. Do you have an issue in getting priority?
<--- Score

54. Who should receive measurement reports?
<--- Score

55. How do you verify your resources?
<--- Score

56. How will you measure your endpoint protection platform market effectiveness?
<--- Score

57. How do you aggregate measures across

priorities?
<--- Score

58. What is your endpoint protection platform market quality cost segregation study?
<--- Score

59. How can a endpoint protection platform market test verify your ideas or assumptions?
<--- Score

60. What are your operating costs?
<--- Score

61. How will you measure success?
<--- Score

62. How will success or failure be measured?
<--- Score

63. What are you verifying?
<--- Score

64. Are the endpoint protection platform market benefits worth its costs?
<--- Score

65. How do you quantify and qualify impacts?
<--- Score

66. What are the endpoint protection platform market investment costs?
<--- Score

67. Where can you go to verify the info?
<--- Score

68. How do you control the overall costs of your work processes?
<--- Score

69. Are indirect costs charged to the endpoint protection platform market program?
<--- Score

70. What are your primary costs, revenues, assets?
<--- Score

71. How do you verify if endpoint protection platform market is built right?
<--- Score

72. What is your decision requirements diagram?
<--- Score

73. What does verifying compliance entail?
<--- Score

74. What relevant entities could be measured?
<--- Score

75. How will costs be allocated?
<--- Score

76. What is an unallowable cost?
<--- Score

77. What harm might be caused?
<--- Score

78. What potential environmental factors impact the endpoint protection platform market effort?

<--- Score

79. How will measures be used to manage and adapt?
<--- Score

80. Why do the measurements/indicators matter?
<--- Score

81. Do the benefits outweigh the costs?
<--- Score

82. Does management have the right priorities among projects?
<--- Score

83. Are you able to realize any cost savings?
<--- Score

84. What are your customers expectations and measures?
<--- Score

85. Who pays the cost?
<--- Score

86. What does your operating model cost?
<--- Score

87. How will effects be measured?
<--- Score

88. Are the measurements objective?
<--- Score

89. What users will be impacted?
<--- Score

90. Have you made assumptions about the shape of the future, particularly its impact on your customers and competitors?
<--- Score

91. What causes innovation to fail or succeed in your organization?
<--- Score

92. What does losing customers cost your organization?
<--- Score

93. What do you measure and why?
<--- Score

94. How frequently do you verify your endpoint protection platform market strategy?
<--- Score

95. Do you have any cost endpoint protection platform market limitation requirements?
<--- Score

96. How frequently do you track endpoint protection platform market measures?
<--- Score

97. What are your key endpoint protection platform market organizational performance measures, including key short and longer-term financial measures?
<--- Score

98. What is the total cost related to deploying

endpoint protection platform market, including any consulting or professional services?
<--- Score

99. How are you verifying it?
<--- Score

100. What is the root cause(s) of the problem?
<--- Score

101. How sensitive must the endpoint protection platform market strategy be to cost?
<--- Score

102. Are actual costs in line with budgeted costs?
<--- Score

103. What evidence is there and what is measured?
<--- Score

104. What measurements are possible, practicable and meaningful?
<--- Score

105. Have design-to-cost goals been established?
<--- Score

106. What causes investor action?
<--- Score

107. What would be a real cause for concern?
<--- Score

108. Are there competing endpoint protection platform market priorities?
<--- Score

109. What measurements are being captured?
<--- Score

110. What methods are feasible and acceptable to estimate the impact of reforms?
<--- Score

111. How do you verify the endpoint protection platform market requirements quality?
<--- Score

112. How are costs allocated?
<--- Score

113. Does the endpoint protection platform market task fit the client's priorities?
<--- Score

114. How do you verify the authenticity of the data and information used?
<--- Score

115. What are the strategic priorities for this year?
<--- Score

116. Do you verify that corrective actions were taken?
<--- Score

117. How can you measure endpoint protection platform market in a systematic way?
<--- Score

118. What are the current costs of the endpoint protection platform market process?
<--- Score

119. How to cause the change?
<--- Score

120. What do people want to verify?
<--- Score

121. Are supply costs steady or fluctuating?
<--- Score

122. What is the total fixed cost?
<--- Score

123. Do you aggressively reward and promote the people who have the biggest impact on creating excellent endpoint protection platform market services/products?
<--- Score

124. How do you prevent mis-estimating cost?
<--- Score

125. Are you aware of what could cause a problem?
<--- Score

126. Which endpoint protection platform market impacts are significant?
<--- Score

127. How do your measurements capture actionable endpoint protection platform market information for use in exceeding your customers expectations and securing your customers engagement?
<--- Score

128. At what cost?

<--- Score

129. Among the endpoint protection platform market product and service cost to be estimated, which is considered hardest to estimate?
<--- Score

130. Where is it measured?
<--- Score

131. How is the value delivered by endpoint protection platform market being measured?
<--- Score

132. Will endpoint protection platform market have an impact on current business continuity, disaster recovery processes and/or infrastructure?
<--- Score

133. Does a endpoint protection platform market quantification method exist?
<--- Score

134. Did you tackle the cause or the symptom?
<--- Score

135. How can you reduce the costs of obtaining inputs?
<--- Score

136. Do you have a flow diagram of what happens?
<--- Score

137. Which costs should be taken into account?
<--- Score

138. Is the solution cost-effective?
<--- Score

139. What is the endpoint protection platform market business impact?
<--- Score

140. How can you reduce costs?
<--- Score

Add up total points for this section:
_____ = Total points for this section

Divided by: _____ (number of statements answered) = _____ Average score for this section

Transfer your score to the endpoint protection platform market Index at the beginning of the Self-Assessment.

CRITERION #4: ANALYZE:

INTENT: Analyze causes, assumptions and hypotheses.

In my belief, the answer to this question is clearly defined:

5 Strongly Agree

4 Agree

3 Neutral

2 Disagree

1 Strongly Disagree

1. What data do you need to collect?
<--- Score

2. What, related to, endpoint protection platform market processes does your organization outsource?
<--- Score

3. How will the endpoint protection platform market data be captured?

<--- Score

4. What successful thing are you doing today that may be blinding you to new growth opportunities?
<--- Score

5. Is there a strict change management process?
<--- Score

6. Do you understand your management processes today?
<--- Score

7. What are the disruptive endpoint protection platform market technologies that enable your organization to radically change your business processes?
<--- Score

8. Record-keeping requirements flow from the records needed as inputs, outputs, controls and for transformation of a endpoint protection platform market process, are the records needed as inputs to the endpoint protection platform market process available?
<--- Score

9. Who will gather what data?
<--- Score

10. How is data used for program management and improvement?
<--- Score

11. How do you identify specific endpoint protection platform market investment opportunities and

emerging trends?
<--- Score

12. What internal processes need improvement?
<--- Score

13. Can you add value to the current endpoint protection platform market decision-making process (largely qualitative) by incorporating uncertainty modeling (more quantitative)?
<--- Score

14. What do you need to qualify?
<--- Score

15. Who will facilitate the team and process?
<--- Score

16. Are all staff in core endpoint protection platform market subjects Highly Qualified?
<--- Score

17. What are your current levels and trends in key endpoint protection platform market measures or indicators of product and process performance that are important to and directly serve your customers?
<--- Score

18. What are the necessary qualifications?
<--- Score

19. Were any designed experiments used to generate additional insight into the data analysis?
<--- Score

20. What endpoint protection platform market data

will be collected?
<--- Score

21. Were Pareto charts (or similar) used to portray the 'heavy hitters' (or key sources of variation)?
<--- Score

22. Who is involved with workflow mapping?
<--- Score

23. How do you implement and manage your work processes to ensure that they meet design requirements?
<--- Score

24. Do you, as a leader, bounce back quickly from setbacks?
<--- Score

25. What qualifications do endpoint protection platform market leaders need?
<--- Score

26. What qualifications are needed?
<--- Score

27. How is endpoint protection platform market data gathered?
<--- Score

28. Did any value-added analysis or 'lean thinking' take place to identify some of the gaps shown on the 'as is' process map?
<--- Score

29. How is the way you as the leader think and process

information affecting your organizational culture?

<--- Score

30. What is the oversight process?

<--- Score

31. What is your organizations process which leads to recognition of value generation?

<--- Score

32. What tools were used to narrow the list of possible causes?

<--- Score

33. Is the performance gap determined?

<--- Score

34. What are the personnel training and qualifications required?

<--- Score

35. What tools were used to generate the list of possible causes?

<--- Score

36. What are the processes for audit reporting and management?

<--- Score

37. Do quality systems drive continuous improvement?

<--- Score

38. What endpoint protection platform market data do you gather or use now?

<--- Score

39. Is the endpoint protection platform market process severely broken such that a re-design is necessary?
<--- Score

40. What qualifications and skills do you need?
<--- Score

41. What will drive endpoint protection platform market change?
<--- Score

42. Have the problem and goal statements been updated to reflect the additional knowledge gained from the analyze phase?
<--- Score

43. What are your current levels and trends in key measures or indicators of endpoint protection platform market product and process performance that are important to and directly serve your customers? How do these results compare with the performance of your competitors and other organizations with similar offerings?
<--- Score

44. What are the best opportunities for value improvement?
<--- Score

45. What conclusions were drawn from the team's data collection and analysis? How did the team reach these conclusions?
<--- Score

46. How has the endpoint protection platform market data been gathered?
<--- Score

47. What did the team gain from developing a sub-process map?
<--- Score

48. What qualifications are necessary?
<--- Score

49. A compounding model resolution with available relevant data can often provide insight towards a solution methodology; which endpoint protection platform market models, tools and techniques are necessary?
<--- Score

50. Was a detailed process map created to amplify critical steps of the 'as is' stakeholder process?
<--- Score

51. Are your outputs consistent?
<--- Score

52. Has data output been validated?
<--- Score

53. Is pre-qualification of suppliers carried out?
<--- Score

54. Are you missing endpoint protection platform market opportunities?
<--- Score

55. Think about some of the processes you undertake

within your organization, which do you own?
<--- Score

56. What endpoint protection platform market data
should be collected?
<--- Score

57. What were the crucial 'moments of truth' on the
process map?
<--- Score

58. How do you measure the operational performance
of your key work systems and processes, including
productivity, cycle time, and other appropriate
measures of process effectiveness, efficiency, and
innovation?
<--- Score

59. Have you defined which data is gathered how?
<--- Score

60. How are outputs preserved and protected?
<--- Score

61. How is the data gathered?
<--- Score

62. What information qualified as important?
<--- Score

63. Was a cause-and-effect diagram used to explore
the different types of causes (or sources of variation)?
<--- Score

64. What data is gathered?
<--- Score

65. How do you use endpoint protection platform market data and information to support organizational decision making and innovation?
<--- Score

66. Did any additional data need to be collected?
<--- Score

67. What does the data say about the performance of the stakeholder process?
<--- Score

68. What is your organizations system for selecting qualified vendors?
<--- Score

69. How much data can be collected in the given timeframe?
<--- Score

70. Where can you get qualified talent today?
<--- Score

71. What is the complexity of the output produced?
<--- Score

72. What other organizational variables, such as reward systems or communication systems, affect the performance of this endpoint protection platform market process?
<--- Score

73. How often will data be collected for measures?
<--- Score

74. Who is involved in the management review process?

<--- Score

75. What endpoint protection platform market metrics are outputs of the process?

<--- Score

76. When should a process be art not science?

<--- Score

77. What process improvements will be needed?

<--- Score

78. How will the change process be managed?

<--- Score

79. What is the endpoint protection platform market Driver?

<--- Score

80. Do your contracts/agreements contain data security obligations?

<--- Score

81. What are the revised rough estimates of the financial savings/opportunity for endpoint protection platform market improvements?

<--- Score

82. How is the endpoint protection platform market Value Stream Mapping managed?

<--- Score

83. Do your leaders quickly bounce back from setbacks?

<--- Score

84. What methods do you use to gather endpoint protection platform market data?
<--- Score

85. Which endpoint protection platform market data should be retained?
<--- Score

86. How does the organization define, manage, and improve its endpoint protection platform market processes?
<--- Score

87. What are evaluation criteria for the output?
<--- Score

88. What process should you select for improvement?
<--- Score

89. Where is the data coming from to measure compliance?
<--- Score

90. Is data and process analysis, root cause analysis and quantifying the gap/opportunity in place?
<--- Score

91. How difficult is it to qualify what endpoint protection platform market ROI is?
<--- Score

92. What resources go in to get the desired output?
<--- Score

93. Who qualifies to gain access to data?

<--- Score

94. Who gets your output?

<--- Score

95. Are endpoint protection platform market changes recognized early enough to be approved through the regular process?

<--- Score

96. Do staff qualifications match your project?

<--- Score

97. Do several people in different organizational units assist with the endpoint protection platform market process?

<--- Score

98. Is the gap/opportunity displayed and communicated in financial terms?

<--- Score

99. What qualifies as competition?

<--- Score

100. What output to create?

<--- Score

101. What is the output?

<--- Score

102. Is the required endpoint protection platform market data gathered?

<--- Score

103. Are all team members qualified for all tasks?
<--- Score

104. How many input/output points does it require?
<--- Score

105. An organizationally feasible system request is one that considers the mission, goals and objectives of the organization, key questions are: is the endpoint protection platform market solution request practical and will it solve a problem or take advantage of an opportunity to achieve company goals?
<--- Score

106. Are gaps between current performance and the goal performance identified?
<--- Score

107. Were there any improvement opportunities identified from the process analysis?
<--- Score

108. What are your outputs?
<--- Score

109. How do your work systems and key work processes relate to and capitalize on your core competencies?
<--- Score

110. Is the final output clearly identified?
<--- Score

111. Is there an established change management process?

<--- Score

112. What is the cost of poor quality as supported by the team's analysis?
<--- Score

113. What quality tools were used to get through the analyze phase?
<--- Score

114. What controls do you have in place to protect data?
<--- Score

115. Do your employees have the opportunity to do what they do best everyday?
<--- Score

116. How can risk management be tied procedurally to process elements?
<--- Score

117. Identify an operational issue in your organization, for example, could a particular task be done more quickly or more efficiently by endpoint protection platform market?
<--- Score

118. Have any additional benefits been identified that will result from closing all or most of the gaps?
<--- Score

119. Should you invest in industry-recognized qualifications?
<--- Score

120. What are your endpoint protection platform market processes?
<--- Score

121. How was the detailed process map generated, verified, and validated?
<--- Score

122. What other jobs or tasks affect the performance of the steps in the endpoint protection platform market process?
<--- Score

123. How will the data be checked for quality?
<--- Score

124. Do you have the authority to produce the output?
<--- Score

125. What kind of crime could a potential new hire have committed that would not only not disqualify him/her from being hired by your organization, but would actually indicate that he/she might be a particularly good fit?
<--- Score

126. What were the financial benefits resulting from any 'ground fruit or low-hanging fruit' (quick fixes)?
<--- Score

127. How do you promote understanding that opportunity for improvement is not criticism of the status quo, or the people who created the status quo?
<--- Score

128. Think about the functions involved in your endpoint protection platform market project, what processes flow from these functions?
<--- Score

129. What types of data do your endpoint protection platform market indicators require?
<--- Score

130. Has an output goal been set?
<--- Score

131. What is the Value Stream Mapping?
<--- Score

132. What are your key performance measures or indicators and in-process measures for the control and improvement of your endpoint protection platform market processes?
<--- Score

133. What are the endpoint protection platform market design outputs?
<--- Score

134. What are the endpoint protection platform market business drivers?
<--- Score

135. What are your best practices for minimizing endpoint protection platform market project risk, while demonstrating incremental value and quick wins throughout the endpoint protection platform market project lifecycle?
<--- Score

Add up total points for this section:

_____ = Total points for this section

Divided by: _____ (number of
statements answered) = _____
Average score for this section

Transfer your score to the endpoint
protection platform market Index at the
beginning of the Self-Assessment.

CRITERION #5: IMPROVE:

INTENT: Develop a practical solution. Innovate, establish and test the solution and to measure the results.

In my belief, the answer to this question is clearly defined:

5 Strongly Agree

4 Agree

3 Neutral

2 Disagree

1 Strongly Disagree

1. How are policy decisions made and where?
<--- Score

2. Who should make the endpoint protection platform market decisions?
<--- Score

3. How do you measure risk?
<--- Score

4. What tools were used to tap into the creativity and encourage 'outside the box' thinking?
<--- Score

5. Do you cover the five essential competencies: Communication, Collaboration,Innovation, Adaptability, and Leadership that improve an organizations ability to leverage the new endpoint protection platform market in a volatile global economy?
<--- Score

6. How will you measure the results?
<--- Score

7. What is the endpoint protection platform market's sustainability risk?
<--- Score

8. What are your current levels and trends in key measures or indicators of workforce and leader development?
<--- Score

9. How does your organization evaluate strategic endpoint protection platform market success?
<--- Score

10. How do you mitigate endpoint protection platform market risk?
<--- Score

11. How can the phases of endpoint protection platform market development be identified?
<--- Score

12. How do you measure improved endpoint protection platform market service perception, and satisfaction?

<--- Score

13. Is there a cost/benefit analysis of optimal solution(s)?

<--- Score

14. What is the risk?

<--- Score

15. Are the key business and technology risks being managed?

<--- Score

16. How do you deal with endpoint protection platform market risk?

<--- Score

17. How does the team improve its work?

<--- Score

18. Is the endpoint protection platform market solution sustainable?

<--- Score

19. Is the endpoint protection platform market risk managed?

<--- Score

20. What tools were most useful during the improve phase?

<--- Score

21. If you could go back in time five years, what decision would you make differently? What is your best guess as to what decision you're making today you might regret five years from now?
<--- Score

22. What strategies for endpoint protection platform market improvement are successful?
<--- Score

23. What is the magnitude of the improvements?
<--- Score

24. Explorations of the frontiers of endpoint protection platform market will help you build influence, improve endpoint protection platform market, optimize decision making, and sustain change, what is your approach?
<--- Score

25. Can you identify any significant risks or exposures to endpoint protection platform market third- parties (vendors, service providers, alliance partners etc) that concern you?
<--- Score

26. How will you recognize and celebrate results?
<--- Score

27. How can you improve endpoint protection platform market?
<--- Score

28. Is the endpoint protection platform market documentation thorough?
<--- Score

29. In the past few months, what is the smallest change you have made that has had the biggest positive result? What was it about that small change that produced the large return?
<--- Score

30. How will you know that you have improved?
<--- Score

31. What actually has to improve and by how much?
<--- Score

32. What attendant changes will need to be made to ensure that the solution is successful?
<--- Score

33. How do you improve productivity?
<--- Score

34. What area needs the greatest improvement?
<--- Score

35. Do vendor agreements bring new compliance risk ?
<--- Score

36. How are endpoint protection platform market risks managed?
<--- Score

37. What is endpoint protection platform market's impact on utilizing the best solution(s)?
<--- Score

38. What is endpoint protection platform market risk?

<--- Score

39. What improvements have been achieved?
<--- Score

40. What should a proof of concept or pilot accomplish?
<--- Score

41. Who will be using the results of the measurement activities?
<--- Score

42. What criteria will you use to assess your endpoint protection platform market risks?
<--- Score

43. What are the affordable endpoint protection platform market risks?
<--- Score

44. Who manages endpoint protection platform market risk?
<--- Score

45. Do you need to do a usability evaluation?
<--- Score

46. What alternative responses are available to manage risk?
<--- Score

47. Who controls the risk?
<--- Score

48. Who will be responsible for making the decisions

to include or exclude requested changes once endpoint protection platform market is underway?
<--- Score

49. Who makes the endpoint protection platform market decisions in your organization?
<--- Score

50. How risky is your organization?
<--- Score

51. What endpoint protection platform market improvements can be made?
<--- Score

52. Is any endpoint protection platform market documentation required?
<--- Score

53. Are risk triggers captured?
<--- Score

54. Have you identified breakpoints and/or risk tolerances that will trigger broad consideration of a potential need for intervention or modification of strategy?
<--- Score

55. What were the criteria for evaluating a endpoint protection platform market pilot?
<--- Score

56. Is there a small-scale pilot for proposed improvement(s)? What conclusions were drawn from the outcomes of a pilot?
<--- Score

57. What resources are required for the improvement efforts?
<--- Score

58. Have you achieved endpoint protection platform market improvements?
<--- Score

59. endpoint protection platform market risk decisions: whose call Is It?
<--- Score

60. What risks do you need to manage?
<--- Score

61. How is continuous improvement applied to risk management?
<--- Score

62. What were the underlying assumptions on the cost-benefit analysis?
<--- Score

63. Who do you report endpoint protection platform market results to?
<--- Score

64. What error proofing will be done to address some of the discrepancies observed in the 'as is' process?
<--- Score

65. What practices helps your organization to develop its capacity to recognize patterns?
<--- Score

66. How do you manage endpoint protection platform market risk?

<--- Score

67. Is there any other endpoint protection platform market solution?

<--- Score

68. What tools do you use once you have decided on a endpoint protection platform market strategy and more importantly how do you choose?

<--- Score

69. Risk Identification: What are the possible risk events your organization faces in relation to endpoint protection platform market?

<--- Score

70. Will the controls trigger any other risks?

<--- Score

71. What communications are necessary to support the implementation of the solution?

<--- Score

72. What is the team's contingency plan for potential problems occurring in implementation?

<--- Score

73. What are the concrete endpoint protection platform market results?

<--- Score

74. Is there a high likelihood that any recommendations will achieve their intended results?

<--- Score

75. Risk factors: what are the characteristics of endpoint protection platform market that make it risky?
<--- Score

76. How can you improve performance?
<--- Score

77. Is the scope clearly documented?
<--- Score

78. Are events managed to resolution?
<--- Score

79. How will you know when its improved?
<--- Score

80. How is knowledge sharing about risk management improved?
<--- Score

81. Who are the endpoint protection platform market decision makers?
<--- Score

82. What current systems have to be understood and/or changed?
<--- Score

83. How scalable is your endpoint protection platform market solution?
<--- Score

84. Are decisions made in a timely manner?

<--- Score

85. When you map the key players in your own work and the types/domains of relationships with them, which relationships do you find easy and which challenging, and why?
<--- Score

86. Was a pilot designed for the proposed solution(s)?
<--- Score

87. Who are the endpoint protection platform market decision-makers?
<--- Score

88. What do you want to improve?
<--- Score

89. How significant is the improvement in the eyes of the end user?
<--- Score

90. Was a endpoint protection platform market charter developed?
<--- Score

91. What went well, what should change, what can improve?
<--- Score

92. How will you know that a change is an improvement?
<--- Score

93. Why improve in the first place?
<--- Score

94. How do you improve endpoint protection platform market service perception, and satisfaction?
<--- Score

95. How do you link measurement and risk?
<--- Score

96. Can you integrate quality management and risk management?
<--- Score

97. Are the risks fully understood, reasonable and manageable?
<--- Score

98. At what point will vulnerability assessments be performed once endpoint protection platform market is put into production (e.g., ongoing Risk Management after implementation)?
<--- Score

99. What can you do to improve?
<--- Score

100. How do you manage and improve your endpoint protection platform market work systems to deliver customer value and achieve organizational success and sustainability?
<--- Score

101. What assumptions are made about the solution and approach?
<--- Score

102. What is the implementation plan?

<--- Score

103. How do you define the solutions' scope?
<--- Score

104. Is the optimal solution selected based on testing and analysis?
<--- Score

105. How do you measure progress and evaluate training effectiveness?
<--- Score

106. Would you develop a endpoint protection platform market Communication Strategy?
<--- Score

107. How do you decide how much to remunerate an employee?
<--- Score

108. How can skill-level changes improve endpoint protection platform market?
<--- Score

109. What needs improvement? Why?
<--- Score

110. Can the solution be designed and implemented within an acceptable time period?
<--- Score

111. Do those selected for the endpoint protection platform market team have a good general understanding of what endpoint protection platform market is all about?

<--- Score

112. How do the endpoint protection platform market results compare with the performance of your competitors and other organizations with similar offerings?
<--- Score

113. Risk events: what are the things that could go wrong?
<--- Score

114. Where do you need endpoint protection platform market improvement?
<--- Score

115. How do you go about comparing endpoint protection platform market approaches/solutions?
<--- Score

116. What lessons, if any, from a pilot were incorporated into the design of the full-scale solution?
<--- Score

117. What does the 'should be' process map/design look like?
<--- Score

118. Is risk periodically assessed?
<--- Score

119. Who will be responsible for documenting the endpoint protection platform market requirements in detail?
<--- Score

120. Is the solution technically practical?
<--- Score

121. Are you assessing endpoint protection platform market and risk?
<--- Score

122. Does a good decision guarantee a good outcome?
<--- Score

123. What to do with the results or outcomes of measurements?
<--- Score

124. Which endpoint protection platform market solution is appropriate?
<--- Score

125. For estimation problems, how do you develop an estimation statement?
<--- Score

126. Were any criteria developed to assist the team in testing and evaluating potential solutions?
<--- Score

127. For decision problems, how do you develop a decision statement?
<--- Score

128. Do you combine technical expertise with business knowledge and endpoint protection platform market Key topics include lifecycles, development approaches, requirements and how to make a business case?

<--- Score

129. To what extent does management recognize endpoint protection platform market as a tool to increase the results?
<--- Score

130. Does the goal represent a desired result that can be measured?
<--- Score

131. How do you keep improving endpoint protection platform market?
<--- Score

132. Are risk management tasks balanced centrally and locally?
<--- Score

133. Is supporting endpoint protection platform market documentation required?
<--- Score

134. What tools were used to evaluate the potential solutions?
<--- Score

Add up total points for this section:
_ _ _ _ _ = Total points for this section

Divided by: _ _ _ _ _ _ (number of statements answered) = _ _ _ _ _ _
Average score for this section

Transfer your score to the endpoint protection platform market Index at the

beginning of the Self-Assessment.

CRITERION #6: CONTROL:

In my belief, the answer to this question is clearly defined:

5 Strongly Agree

4 Agree

3 Neutral

2 Disagree

1 Strongly Disagree

1. How do senior leaders actions reflect a commitment to the organizations endpoint protection platform market values?
<--- Score

2. What is the recommended frequency of auditing?
<--- Score

3. What are customers monitoring?

<--- Score

4. Has the improved process and its steps been standardized?
<--- Score

5. How will the process owner and team be able to hold the gains?
<--- Score

6. What are the known security controls?
<--- Score

7. What quality tools were useful in the control phase?
<--- Score

8. Are the planned controls in place?
<--- Score

9. How do you plan for the cost of succession?
<--- Score

10. What is the standard for acceptable endpoint protection platform market performance?
<--- Score

11. Has the endpoint protection platform market value of standards been quantified?
<--- Score

12. Are there documented procedures?
<--- Score

13. Are you measuring, monitoring and predicting endpoint protection platform market activities to optimize operations and profitability, and enhancing

outcomes?
<--- Score

14. How do you establish and deploy modified action plans if circumstances require a shift in plans and rapid execution of new plans?
<--- Score

15. What are your results for key measures or indicators of the accomplishment of your endpoint protection platform market strategy and action plans, including building and strengthening core competencies?
<--- Score

16. Is there a standardized process?
<--- Score

17. How do you plan on providing proper recognition and disclosure of supporting companies?
<--- Score

18. How will input, process, and output variables be checked to detect for sub-optimal conditions?
<--- Score

19. Are operating procedures consistent?
<--- Score

20. How likely is the current endpoint protection platform market plan to come in on schedule or on budget?
<--- Score

21. Act/Adjust: What Do you Need to Do Differently?

<--- Score

22. In the case of a endpoint protection platform market project, the criteria for the audit derive from implementation objectives, an audit of a endpoint protection platform market project involves assessing whether the recommendations outlined for implementation have been met, can you track that any endpoint protection platform market project is implemented as planned, and is it working?
<--- Score

23. Are suggested corrective/restorative actions indicated on the response plan for known causes to problems that might surface?
<--- Score

24. What key inputs and outputs are being measured on an ongoing basis?
<--- Score

25. Can you adapt and adjust to changing endpoint protection platform market situations?
<--- Score

26. Will your goals reflect your program budget?
<--- Score

27. How do your controls stack up?
<--- Score

28. What other systems, operations, processes, and infrastructures (hiring practices, staffing, training, incentives/rewards, metrics/dashboards/scorecards, etc.) need updates, additions, changes, or deletions in order to facilitate knowledge transfer and

improvements?

<--- Score

29. Do you monitor the endpoint protection platform market decisions made and fine tune them as they evolve?

<--- Score

30. How do you monitor usage and cost?

<--- Score

31. Is there a recommended audit plan for routine surveillance inspections of endpoint protection platform market's gains?

<--- Score

32. Can support from partners be adjusted?

<--- Score

33. What can you control?

<--- Score

34. Is the endpoint protection platform market test/ monitoring cost justified?

<--- Score

35. Is there a control plan in place for sustaining improvements (short and long-term)?

<--- Score

36. How do controls support value?

<--- Score

37. Does endpoint protection platform market appropriately measure and monitor risk?

<--- Score

38. What should you measure to verify efficiency gains?
<--- Score

39. Are the planned controls working?
<--- Score

40. What do your reports reflect?
<--- Score

41. How do you select, collect, align, and integrate endpoint protection platform market data and information for tracking daily operations and overall organizational performance, including progress relative to strategic objectives and action plans?
<--- Score

42. Is there an action plan in case of emergencies?
<--- Score

43. Will any special training be provided for results interpretation?
<--- Score

44. Does the endpoint protection platform market performance meet the customer's requirements?
<--- Score

45. How will report readings be checked to effectively monitor performance?
<--- Score

46. What are you attempting to measure/monitor?
<--- Score

47. How is change control managed?
<--- Score

48. What is the control/monitoring plan?
<--- Score

49. How will new or emerging customer needs/ requirements be checked/communicated to orient the process toward meeting the new specifications and continually reducing variation?
<--- Score

50. Who is the endpoint protection platform market process owner?
<--- Score

51. What are the critical parameters to watch?
<--- Score

52. Are documented procedures clear and easy to follow for the operators?
<--- Score

53. Does a troubleshooting guide exist or is it needed?
<--- Score

54. Is a response plan in place for when the input, process, or output measures indicate an 'out-of-control' condition?
<--- Score

55. You may have created your quality measures at a time when you lacked resources, technology wasn't up to the required standard, or low service levels were the industry norm. Have those circumstances changed?

<--- Score

56. Are the endpoint protection platform market standards challenging?
<--- Score

57. Do you monitor the effectiveness of your endpoint protection platform market activities?
<--- Score

58. How will the process owner verify improvement in present and future sigma levels, process capabilities?
<--- Score

59. How will the day-to-day responsibilities for monitoring and continual improvement be transferred from the improvement team to the process owner?
<--- Score

60. What adjustments to the strategies are needed?
<--- Score

61. What are the key elements of your endpoint protection platform market performance improvement system, including your evaluation, organizational learning, and innovation processes?
<--- Score

62. Have new or revised work instructions resulted?
<--- Score

63. Who sets the endpoint protection platform market standards?
<--- Score

64. Does job training on the documented procedures need to be part of the process team's education and training?
<--- Score

65. Who is going to spread your message?
<--- Score

66. How will endpoint protection platform market decisions be made and monitored?
<--- Score

67. How widespread is its use?
<--- Score

68. Are controls in place and consistently applied?
<--- Score

69. Is reporting being used or needed?
<--- Score

70. Is there a documented and implemented monitoring plan?
<--- Score

71. Is a response plan established and deployed?
<--- Score

72. What endpoint protection platform market standards are applicable?
<--- Score

73. What do you measure to verify effectiveness gains?
<--- Score

74. Where do ideas that reach policy makers and planners as proposals for endpoint protection platform market strengthening and reform actually originate?
<--- Score

75. What is the best design framework for endpoint protection platform market organization now that, in a post industrial-age if the top-down, command and control model is no longer relevant?
<--- Score

76. What other areas of the group might benefit from the endpoint protection platform market team's improvements, knowledge, and learning?
<--- Score

77. Is new knowledge gained imbedded in the response plan?
<--- Score

78. How can you best use all of your knowledge repositories to enhance learning and sharing?
<--- Score

79. Does the response plan contain a definite closed loop continual improvement scheme (e.g., plan-do-check-act)?
<--- Score

80. Who controls critical resources?
<--- Score

81. How do you encourage people to take control and responsibility?
<--- Score

82. Will existing staff require re-training, for example, to learn new business processes?
<--- Score

83. How is endpoint protection platform market project cost planned, managed, monitored?
<--- Score

84. How might the group capture best practices and lessons learned so as to leverage improvements?
<--- Score

85. Are new process steps, standards, and documentation ingrained into normal operations?
<--- Score

86. Will the team be available to assist members in planning investigations?
<--- Score

87. Is there a endpoint protection platform market Communication plan covering who needs to get what information when?
<--- Score

88. How will you measure your QA plan's effectiveness?
<--- Score

89. What is your theory of human motivation, and how does your compensation plan fit with that view?
<--- Score

90. What should the next improvement project be that is related to endpoint protection platform

market?

<--- Score

91. Do the endpoint protection platform market decisions you make today help people and the planet tomorrow?

<--- Score

92. Are pertinent alerts monitored, analyzed and distributed to appropriate personnel?

<--- Score

93. Who will be in control?

<--- Score

94. Is there documentation that will support the successful operation of the improvement?

<--- Score

95. Is knowledge gained on process shared and institutionalized?

<--- Score

96. What do you stand for--and what are you against?

<--- Score

97. How do you spread information?

<--- Score

98. Who has control over resources?

<--- Score

99. Is there a transfer of ownership and knowledge to process owner and process team tasked with the responsibilities.

<--- Score

100. What is your plan to assess your security risks?

<--- Score

Add up total points for this section:
_ _ _ _ _   = Total points for this section

Divided by: _ _ _ _ _ _ (number of
statements answered) = _ _ _ _ _ _
Average score for this section

Transfer your score to the endpoint
protection platform market Index at the
beginning of the Self-Assessment.

CRITERION #7: SUSTAIN:

INTENT: Retain the benefits.

In my belief, the answer to this question is clearly defined:

5 Strongly Agree

4 Agree

3 Neutral

2 Disagree

1 Strongly Disagree

1. Is there a work around that you can use?
<--- Score

2. What is the craziest thing you can do?
<--- Score

3. Is it economical; do you have the time and money?
<--- Score

4. At what moment would you think; Will I get fired?

<--- Score

5. What is your competitive advantage?
<--- Score

6. Can you do all this work?
<--- Score

7. Who will be responsible for deciding whether endpoint protection platform market goes ahead or not after the initial investigations?
<--- Score

8. How long will it take to change?
<--- Score

9. Is the endpoint protection platform market organization completing tasks effectively and efficiently?
<--- Score

10. Why not do endpoint protection platform market?
<--- Score

11. What you are going to do to affect the numbers?
<--- Score

12. How do you proactively clarify deliverables and endpoint protection platform market quality expectations?
<--- Score

13. What is your BATNA (best alternative to a negotiated agreement)?
<--- Score

14. What is a feasible sequencing of reform initiatives over time?
<--- Score

15. Are the criteria for selecting recommendations stated?
<--- Score

16. What is the recommended frequency of auditing?
<--- Score

17. What is something you believe that nearly no one agrees with you on?
<--- Score

18. Who are your customers?
<--- Score

19. How do you keep records, of what?
<--- Score

20. Is the impact that endpoint protection platform market has shown?
<--- Score

21. What endpoint protection platform market modifications can you make work for you?
<--- Score

22. Is a endpoint protection platform market team work effort in place?
<--- Score

23. What trophy do you want on your mantle?
<--- Score

24. How do you determine the key elements that affect endpoint protection platform market workforce satisfaction, how are these elements determined for different workforce groups and segments?
<--- Score

25. What is effective endpoint protection platform market?
<--- Score

26. Think of your endpoint protection platform market project, what are the main functions?
<--- Score

27. Do you think endpoint protection platform market accomplishes the goals you expect it to accomplish?
<--- Score

28. How can you incorporate support to ensure safe and effective use of endpoint protection platform market into the services that you provide?
<--- Score

29. Who is the main stakeholder, with ultimate responsibility for driving endpoint protection platform market forward?
<--- Score

30. What are strategies for increasing support and reducing opposition?
<--- Score

31. Marketing budgets are tighter, consumers are more skeptical, and social media has changed forever the way we talk about endpoint protection platform

market, how do you gain traction?
<--- Score

32. How do you deal with endpoint protection platform market changes?
<--- Score

33. How do you ensure that implementations of endpoint protection platform market products are done in a way that ensures safety?
<--- Score

34. Do you have past endpoint protection platform market successes?
<--- Score

35. How can you become more high-tech but still be high touch?
<--- Score

36. How do you keep the momentum going?
<--- Score

37. What is the kind of project structure that would be appropriate for your endpoint protection platform market project, should it be formal and complex, or can it be less formal and relatively simple?
<--- Score

38. What will be the consequences to the stakeholder (financial, reputation etc) if endpoint protection platform market does not go ahead or fails to deliver the objectives?
<--- Score

39. Which endpoint protection platform market goals

are the most important?

<--- Score

40. Is there any reason to believe the opposite of my current belief?

<--- Score

41. What may be the consequences for the performance of an organization if all stakeholders are not consulted regarding endpoint protection platform market?

<--- Score

42. What are you trying to prove to yourself, and how might it be hijacking your life and business success?

<--- Score

43. What did you miss in the interview for the worst hire you ever made?

<--- Score

44. Are there any activities that you can take off your to do list?

<--- Score

45. What is the funding source for this project?

<--- Score

46. Who will manage the integration of tools?

<--- Score

47. Are you paying enough attention to the partners your company depends on to succeed?

<--- Score

48. What is the source of the strategies for endpoint protection platform market strengthening and reform?
<--- Score

49. If you were responsible for initiating and implementing major changes in your organization, what steps might you take to ensure acceptance of those changes?
<--- Score

50. How do you foster the skills, knowledge, talents, attributes, and characteristics you want to have?
<--- Score

51. What are current endpoint protection platform market paradigms?
<--- Score

52. What endpoint protection platform market skills are most important?
<--- Score

53. What goals did you miss?
<--- Score

54. How can you become the company that would put you out of business?
<--- Score

55. Do you know who is a friend or a foe?
<--- Score

56. What are the business goals endpoint protection platform market is aiming to achieve?
<--- Score

57. What unique value proposition (UVP) do you offer?
<--- Score

58. How will you insure seamless interoperability of endpoint protection platform market moving forward?
<--- Score

59. Operational - will it work?
<--- Score

60. Who will determine interim and final deadlines?
<--- Score

61. What business benefits will endpoint protection platform market goals deliver if achieved?
<--- Score

62. Has implementation been effective in reaching specified objectives so far?
<--- Score

63. Is a endpoint protection platform market breakthrough on the horizon?
<--- Score

64. How do you transition from the baseline to the target?
<--- Score

65. If you weren't already in this business, would you enter it today? And if not, what are you going to do about it?

<--- Score

66. Do you know what you are doing? And who do you call if you don't?
<--- Score

67. Are your responses positive or negative?
<--- Score

68. How are you doing compared to your industry?
<--- Score

69. How do you engage the workforce, in addition to satisfying them?
<--- Score

70. What was the last experiment you ran?
<--- Score

71. Will there be any necessary staff changes (redundancies or new hires)?
<--- Score

72. Why is it important to have senior management support for a endpoint protection platform market project?
<--- Score

73. How do you foster innovation?
<--- Score

74. Were lessons learned captured and communicated?
<--- Score

75. Is endpoint protection platform market

dependent on the successful delivery of a current project?

<--- Score

76. What stupid rule would you most like to kill?

<--- Score

77. What are the rules and assumptions your industry operates under? What if the opposite were true?

<--- Score

78. Is there any existing endpoint protection platform market governance structure?

<--- Score

79. How do you govern and fulfill your societal responsibilities?

<--- Score

80. Will it be accepted by users?

<--- Score

81. How much contingency will be available in the budget?

<--- Score

82. Do you think you know, or do you know you know ?

<--- Score

83. How do you set endpoint protection platform market stretch targets and how do you get people to not only participate in setting these stretch targets but also that they strive to achieve these?

<--- Score

84. Are you relevant? Will you be relevant five years from now? Ten?
<--- Score

85. Are assumptions made in endpoint protection platform market stated explicitly?
<--- Score

86. What are the usability implications of endpoint protection platform market actions?
<--- Score

87. Are you satisfied with your current role? If not, what is missing from it?
<--- Score

88. Can the schedule be done in the given time?
<--- Score

89. What happens if you do not have enough funding?
<--- Score

90. How do you assess the endpoint protection platform market pitfalls that are inherent in implementing it?
<--- Score

91. What would you recommend your friend do if he/she were facing this dilemma?
<--- Score

92. Which individuals, teams or departments will be involved in endpoint protection platform market?

<--- Score

93. What would have to be true for the option on the table to be the best possible choice?
<--- Score

94. Who is responsible for errors?
<--- Score

95. Are the assumptions believable and achievable?
<--- Score

96. Why will customers want to buy your organizations products/services?
<--- Score

97. What are the performance and scale of the endpoint protection platform market tools?
<--- Score

98. How is implementation research currently incorporated into each of your goals?
<--- Score

99. What is the purpose of endpoint protection platform market in relation to the mission?
<--- Score

100. What could happen if you do not do it?
<--- Score

101. How do you stay inspired?
<--- Score

102. Who do we want your customers to become?
<--- Score

103. What are the gaps in your knowledge and experience?
<--- Score

104. Why should you adopt a endpoint protection platform market framework?
<--- Score

105. Can you break it down?
<--- Score

106. How important is endpoint protection platform market to the user organizations mission?
<--- Score

107. What have been your experiences in defining long range endpoint protection platform market goals?
<--- Score

108. How do you cross-sell and up-sell your endpoint protection platform market success?
<--- Score

109. Do you say no to customers for no reason?
<--- Score

110. What role does communication play in the success or failure of a endpoint protection platform market project?
<--- Score

111. What are the short and long-term endpoint protection platform market goals?

<--- Score

112. Would you rather sell to knowledgeable and informed customers or to uninformed customers?
<--- Score

113. What is your endpoint protection platform market strategy?
<--- Score

114. When information truly is ubiquitous, when reach and connectivity are completely global, when computing resources are infinite, and when a whole new set of impossibilities are not only possible, but happening, what will that do to your business?
<--- Score

115. What is it like to work for you?
<--- Score

116. If you find that you havent accomplished one of the goals for one of the steps of the endpoint protection platform market strategy, what will you do to fix it?
<--- Score

117. Why should people listen to you?
<--- Score

118. If your customer were your grandmother, would you tell her to buy what you're selling?
<--- Score

119. How do you make it meaningful in connecting endpoint protection platform market with what users do day-to-day?

<--- Score

120. What is the overall business strategy?
<--- Score

121. Do you have an implicit bias for capital investments over people investments?
<--- Score

122. What management system can you use to leverage the endpoint protection platform market experience, ideas, and concerns of the people closest to the work to be done?
<--- Score

123. Do you have the right capabilities and capacities?
<--- Score

124. What must you excel at?
<--- Score

125. What are the long-term endpoint protection platform market goals?
<--- Score

126. Do you have enough freaky customers in your portfolio pushing you to the limit day in and day out?
<--- Score

127. What are your personal philosophies regarding endpoint protection platform market and how do they influence your work?
<--- Score

128. How do you know if you are successful?
<--- Score

129. If your company went out of business tomorrow, would anyone who doesn't get a paycheck here care?

<--- Score

130. Do you have the right people on the bus?

<--- Score

131. Did your employees make progress today?

<--- Score

132. What threat is endpoint protection platform market addressing?

<--- Score

133. Why do and why don't your customers like your organization?

<--- Score

134. Who uses your product in ways you never expected?

<--- Score

135. Whom among your colleagues do you trust, and for what?

<--- Score

136. How does endpoint protection platform market integrate with other stakeholder initiatives?

<--- Score

137. Is endpoint protection platform market realistic, or are you setting yourself up for failure?

<--- Score

138. How do customers see your organization?
<--- Score

139. Who are the key stakeholders?
<--- Score

140. Instead of going to current contacts for new ideas, what if you reconnected with dormant contacts--the people you used to know? If you were going reactivate a dormant tie, who would it be?
<--- Score

141. Can you maintain your growth without detracting from the factors that have contributed to your success?
<--- Score

142. Which models, tools and techniques are necessary?
<--- Score

143. Who is responsible for ensuring appropriate resources (time, people and money) are allocated to endpoint protection platform market?
<--- Score

144. Are new benefits received and understood?
<--- Score

145. Why is endpoint protection platform market important for you now?
<--- Score

146. How much does endpoint protection platform market help?

<--- Score

147. If you do not follow, then how to lead?
<--- Score

148. What does your signature ensure?
<--- Score

149. How do you go about securing endpoint protection platform market?
<--- Score

150. Who do you want your customers to become?
<--- Score

151. What are the top 3 things at the forefront of your endpoint protection platform market agendas for the next 3 years?
<--- Score

152. What have you done to protect your business from competitive encroachment?
<--- Score

153. Is your strategy driving your strategy? Or is the way in which you allocate resources driving your strategy?
<--- Score

154. Who have you, as a company, historically been when you've been at your best?
<--- Score

155. Who are four people whose careers you have enhanced?
<--- Score

156. How do you manage endpoint protection platform market Knowledge Management (KM)?
<--- Score

157. How can you negotiate endpoint protection platform market successfully with a stubborn boss, an irate client, or a deceitful coworker?
<--- Score

158. What are the barriers to increased endpoint protection platform market production?
<--- Score

159. How do you track customer value, profitability or financial return, organizational success, and sustainability?
<--- Score

160. What projects are going on in the organization today, and what resources are those projects using from the resource pools?
<--- Score

161. What trouble can you get into?
<--- Score

162. What knowledge, skills and characteristics mark a good endpoint protection platform market project manager?
<--- Score

163. What do we do when new problems arise?
<--- Score

164. If there were zero limitations, what would you do

differently?
<--- Score

165. If you got fired and a new hire took your place, what would she do different?
<--- Score

166. If you had to leave your organization for a year and the only communication you could have with employees/colleagues was a single paragraph, what would you write?
<--- Score

167. Political -is anyone trying to undermine this project?
<--- Score

168. What are the potential basics of endpoint protection platform market fraud?
<--- Score

169. Do you see more potential in people than they do in themselves?
<--- Score

170. What should you stop doing?
<--- Score

171. Are all key stakeholders present at all Structured Walkthroughs?
<--- Score

172. Who will provide the final approval of endpoint protection platform market deliverables?
<--- Score

173. If you had to rebuild your organization without any traditional competitive advantages (i.e., no killer technology, promising research, innovative product/service delivery model, etcetera), how would your people have to approach their work and collaborate together in order to create the necessary conditions for success?
<--- Score

174. Who is responsible for endpoint protection platform market?
<--- Score

175. What is an unauthorized commitment?
<--- Score

176. What new services of functionality will be implemented next with endpoint protection platform market ?
<--- Score

177. How do senior leaders deploy your organizations vision and values through your leadership system, to the workforce, to key suppliers and partners, and to customers and other stakeholders, as appropriate?
<--- Score

178. What are the essentials of internal endpoint protection platform market management?
<--- Score

179. What is your formula for success in endpoint protection platform market ?
<--- Score

180. Where can you break convention?
<--- Score

181. How do you lead with endpoint protection platform market in mind?
<--- Score

182. What happens at your organization when people fail?
<--- Score

183. What is the big endpoint protection platform market idea?
<--- Score

184. Who do you think the world wants your organization to be?
<--- Score

185. What relationships among endpoint protection platform market trends do you perceive?
<--- Score

186. Is your basic point _____ or _____?
<--- Score

187. How do you provide a safe environment -physically and emotionally?
<--- Score

188. How will you know that the endpoint protection platform market project has been successful?
<--- Score

189. What are the success criteria that will indicate

that endpoint protection platform market objectives have been met and the benefits delivered?
<--- Score

190. Do you feel that more should be done in the endpoint protection platform market area?
<--- Score

191. Are you making progress, and are you making progress as endpoint protection platform market leaders?
<--- Score

192. What are your most important goals for the strategic endpoint protection platform market objectives?
<--- Score

193. Have new benefits been realized?
<--- Score

194. How do you maintain endpoint protection platform market's Integrity?
<--- Score

195. How do you accomplish your long range endpoint protection platform market goals?
<--- Score

196. Do endpoint protection platform market rules make a reasonable demand on a users capabilities?
<--- Score

197. What one word do you want to own in the minds of your customers, employees, and partners?

<--- Score

198. What are the key enablers to make this endpoint protection platform market move?
<--- Score

199. Are you maintaining a past–present–future perspective throughout the endpoint protection platform market discussion?
<--- Score

200. Who, on the executive team or the board, has spoken to a customer recently?
<--- Score

201. What are internal and external endpoint protection platform market relations?
<--- Score

202. How will you ensure you get what you expected?
<--- Score

203. How likely is it that a customer would recommend your company to a friend or colleague?
<--- Score

204. How do you listen to customers to obtain actionable information?
<--- Score

205. In retrospect, of the projects that you pulled the plug on, what percent do you wish had been allowed to keep going, and what percent do you wish had ended earlier?

<--- Score

206. Are you changing as fast as the world around you?
<--- Score

207. Is maximizing endpoint protection platform market protection the same as minimizing endpoint protection platform market loss?
<--- Score

208. What information is critical to your organization that your executives are ignoring?
<--- Score

209. To whom do you add value?
<--- Score

210. What are the challenges?
<--- Score

211. What is the overall talent health of your organization as a whole at senior levels, and for each organization reporting to a member of the Senior Leadership Team?
<--- Score

212. If no one would ever find out about your accomplishments, how would you lead differently?
<--- Score

213. What counts that you are not counting?
<--- Score

214. Have benefits been optimized with all key stakeholders?

<--- Score

Add up total points for this section:
_____ = Total points for this section

Divided by: _____ (number of
statements answered) = _____
Average score for this section

Transfer your score to the endpoint
protection platform market Index at the
beginning of the Self-Assessment.

Endpoint Protection Platform Market and Managing Projects, Criteria for Project Managers:

1.0 Initiating Process Group: Endpoint Protection Platform Market

1. Are the changes in your Endpoint Protection Platform Market project being formally requested, analyzed, and approved by the appropriate decision makers?

2. If the risk event occurs, what will you do?

3. Professionals want to know what is expected from them what are the deliverables?

4. Contingency planning. if a risk event occurs, what will you do?

5. Who is performing the work of the Endpoint Protection Platform Market project?

6. Who are the Endpoint Protection Platform Market project stakeholders?

7. Did the Endpoint Protection Platform Market project team have the right skills?

8. What were things that you did well, and could improve, and how?

9. Do you understand the quality and control criteria that must be achieved for successful Endpoint Protection Platform Market project completion?

10. How should needs be met?

11. Are the Endpoint Protection Platform Market

project team and stakeholders meeting regularly and using a meeting agenda and taking notes to accurately document what is being covered and what happened in the weekly meetings?

12. What are the tools and techniques to be used in each phase?

13. What are the pressing issues of the hour?

14. Have you evaluated the teams performance and asked for feedback?

15. How will you do it?

16. What areas were overlooked on this Endpoint Protection Platform Market project?

17. What do you need to do?

18. Who does what?

19. Who supports, improves, and oversees standardized processes related to the Endpoint Protection Platform Market projects program?

20. How well did you do?

1.1 Project Charter: Endpoint Protection Platform Market

21. If finished, on what date did it finish?

22. What material?

23. Who is the Endpoint Protection Platform Market project Manager?

24. Why executive support?

25. What are the known stakeholder requirements?

26. Is it an improvement over existing products?

27. Did your Endpoint Protection Platform Market project ask for this?

28. What are the assigned resources?

29. When do you use a Endpoint Protection Platform Market project Charter?

30. What is the justification?

31. What is in it for you?

32. Why use a Endpoint Protection Platform Market project charter?

33. Why is it important?

34. What goes into your Endpoint Protection Platform Market project Charter?

35. What are the assumptions?

36. Where does all this information come from?

37. How high should you set your goals?

38. Review the general mission What system will be affected by the improvement efforts?

39. What outcome, in measureable terms, are you hoping to accomplish?

40. When is a charter needed?

1.2 Stakeholder Register: Endpoint Protection Platform Market

41. Who wants to talk about Security?

42. How should employers make voices heard?

43. How much influence do they have on the Endpoint Protection Platform Market project?

44. Is your organization ready for change?

45. How will reports be created?

46. Who are the stakeholders?

47. Who is managing stakeholder engagement?

48. What are the major Endpoint Protection Platform Market project milestones requiring communications or providing communications opportunities?

49. How big is the gap?

50. What & Why?

51. What opportunities exist to provide communications?

52. What is the power of the stakeholder?

1.3 Stakeholder Analysis Matrix: Endpoint Protection Platform Market

53. Who influences whom?

54. Which resources are required?

55. What mechanisms are proposed to monitor and measure Endpoint Protection Platform Market project performance in terms of social development outcomes?

56. Who has the power to influence the outcomes of the work?

57. Processes and systems, etc?

58. Arena: in what fields are the actors active, where are they present?

59. What are the key services, contractual arrangements, or other relationships between stakeholder groups?

60. Are you going to weigh the stakeholders?

61. Who will be affected by the work?

62. Competitive advantages?

63. Information and research?

64. How much do resources cost?

65. Do recommendations include actions to address any differential distribution of impacts?

66. What are the mechanisms of public and social accountability, and how can they be made better?

67. Continuity, supply chain robustness?

68. What is the range you need to look at?

69. How will the Endpoint Protection Platform Market project benefit them?

70. Market developments?

71. Inoculations or payment to receive them?

72. What advantages do your organizations stakeholders have?

2.0 Planning Process Group: Endpoint Protection Platform Market

73. What type of estimation method are you using?

74. Have more efficient (sensitive) and appropriate measures been adopted to respond to the political and socio-cultural problems identified?

75. If a risk event occurs, what will you do?

76. To what extent are the visions and actions of the partners consistent or divergent with regard to the program?

77. How well do the team follow the chosen processes?

78. How do you integrate Endpoint Protection Platform Market project Planning with the Iterative/ Evolutionary SDLC?

79. Are there efficient coordination mechanisms to avoid overloading the counterparts, participating stakeholders?

80. Mitigate. what will you do to minimize the impact should a risk event occur?

81. What makes your Endpoint Protection Platform Market project successful?

82. What input will you be required to provide the

Endpoint Protection Platform Market project team?

83. Explanation: is what the Endpoint Protection Platform Market project intents to solve a hard question?

84. To what extent are the participating departments coordinating with each other?

85. If a task is partitionable, is this a sufficient condition to reduce the Endpoint Protection Platform Market project duration?

86. To what extent is the program helping to influence your organizations policy framework?

87. In what way has the Endpoint Protection Platform Market project come up with innovative measures for problem-solving?

88. How are the principles of aid effectiveness (ownership, alignment, management for development results and mutual responsibility) being applied in the Endpoint Protection Platform Market project?

89. How will it affect you?

90. To what extent has a PMO contributed to raising the quality of the design of the Endpoint Protection Platform Market project?

91. Endpoint Protection Platform Market project assessment; why did you do this Endpoint Protection Platform Market project?

2.1 Project Management Plan: Endpoint Protection Platform Market

92. What is Endpoint Protection Platform Market project scope management?

93. Did the planning effort collaborate to develop solutions that integrate expertise, policies, programs, and Endpoint Protection Platform Market projects across entities?

94. Do the proposed changes from the Endpoint Protection Platform Market project include any significant risks to safety?

95. Is mitigation authorized or recommended?

96. What did not work so well?

97. What data/reports/tools/etc. do program managers need?

98. What went wrong?

99. Are comparable cost estimates used for comparing, screening and selecting alternative plans, and has a reasonable cost estimate been developed for the recommended plan?

100. How well are you able to manage your risk?

101. Does the selected plan protect privacy?

102. What if, for example, the positive direction and vision of your organization causes expected trends to change resulting in greater need than expected?

103. Are there any Client staffing expectations?

104. Does the implementation plan have an appropriate division of responsibilities?

105. Why Change?

106. What went right?

2.2 Scope Management Plan: Endpoint Protection Platform Market

107. Timeline and milestones?

108. Is there a set of procedures defining the scope, procedures, and deliverables defining quality control?

109. Has a quality assurance plan been developed for the Endpoint Protection Platform Market project?

110. Are the results of quality assurance reviews provided to affected groups & individuals?

111. Is the schedule updated on a periodic basis?

112. Are the payment terms being followed?

113. Can the Endpoint Protection Platform Market project team do several activities in parallel?

114. Has a structured approach been used to break work effort into manageable components (WBS)?

115. What are the risks that could significantly affect the schedule of the Endpoint Protection Platform Market project?

116. Does the Endpoint Protection Platform Market project team have the skills necessary to successfully complete current Endpoint Protection Platform Market project(s) and support the application?

117. Are changes in scope (deliverable commitments) agreed to by all affected groups & individuals?

118. Is an industry recognized mechanized support tool(s) being used for Endpoint Protection Platform Market project scheduling & tracking?

119. Is quality monitored from the perspective of the customers needs and expectations?

120. Are trade-offs between accepting the risk and mitigating the risk identified?

121. Has the Endpoint Protection Platform Market project manager been identified?

122. Have the procedures for identifying budget variances been followed?

123. Are procurement deliverables arriving on time and to specification?

124. Time estimation – how much time will be needed?

125. Why is a scope management plan important?

126. Is there general agreement & acceptance of the current status and progress of the Endpoint Protection Platform Market project?

2.3 Requirements Management Plan: Endpoint Protection Platform Market

127. Who is responsible for monitoring and tracking the Endpoint Protection Platform Market project requirements?

128. How knowledgeable is the primary Stakeholder(s) in the proposed application area?

129. How detailed should the Endpoint Protection Platform Market project get?

130. Has the requirements team been instructed in the Change Control process?

131. Could inaccurate or incomplete requirements in this Endpoint Protection Platform Market project create a serious risk for the business?

132. Do you have an appropriate arrangement for meetings?

133. What is the earliest finish date for this Endpoint Protection Platform Market project if it is scheduled to start on ...?

134. In case of software development; Should you have a test for each code module?

135. Do you know which stakeholders will participate in the requirements effort?

136. Who will perform the analysis?

137. Will the Endpoint Protection Platform Market project requirements become approved in writing?

138. Did you avoid subjective, flowery or non-specific statements?

139. Who will finally present the work or product(s) for acceptance?

140. Business analysis scope?

141. Who came up with this requirement?

142. Should you include sub-activities?

143. How will bidders price evaluations be done, by deliverables, phases, or in a big bang?

144. Is requirements work dependent on any other specific Endpoint Protection Platform Market project or non-Endpoint Protection Platform Market project activities (e.g. funding, approvals, procurement)?

145. What are you counting on?

146. Will you perform a Requirements Risk assessment and develop a plan to deal with risks?

2.4 Requirements Documentation: Endpoint Protection Platform Market

147. Where do you define what is a customer, what are the attributes of customer?

148. What facilities must be supported by the system?

149. Who is interacting with the system?

150. Are all functions required by the customer included?

151. How does the proposed Endpoint Protection Platform Market project contribute to the overall objectives of your organization?

152. Have the benefits identified with the system being identified clearly?

153. If applicable; are there issues linked with the fact that this is an offshore Endpoint Protection Platform Market project?

154. What are the attributes of a customer?

155. Basic work/business process; high-level, what is being touched?

156. Who provides requirements?

157. Validity. does the system provide the functions which best support the customers needs?

158. How does what is being described meet the business need?

159. What happens when requirements are wrong?

160. How do you know when a Requirement is accurate enough?

161. Do technical resources exist?

162. Completeness. are all functions required by the customer included?

163. Is new technology needed?

164. Is the requirement realistically testable?

165. What is a show stopper in the requirements?

166. How will they be documented / shared?

2.5 Requirements Traceability Matrix: Endpoint Protection Platform Market

167. What is the WBS?

168. How do you manage scope?

169. What percentage of Endpoint Protection Platform Market projects are producing traceability matrices between requirements and other work products?

170. How will it affect the stakeholders personally in career?

171. Do you have a clear understanding of all subcontracts in place?

172. Is there a requirements traceability process in place?

173. What are the chronologies, contingencies, consequences, criteria?

174. Describe the process for approving requirements so they can be added to the traceability matrix and Endpoint Protection Platform Market project work can be performed. Will the Endpoint Protection Platform Market project requirements become approved in writing?

175. How small is small enough?

176. Why do you manage scope?

177. Why use a WBS?

178. Will you use a Requirements Traceability Matrix?

2.6 Project Scope Statement: Endpoint Protection Platform Market

179. Do you anticipate new stakeholders joining the Endpoint Protection Platform Market project over time?

180. If you were to write a list of what should not be included in the scope statement, what are the things that you would recommend be described as out-of-scope?

181. Are there adequate Endpoint Protection Platform Market project control systems?

182. What are the major deliverables of the Endpoint Protection Platform Market project?

183. Is the Endpoint Protection Platform Market project sponsor function identified and defined?

184. Have you been able to easily identify success criteria and create objective measurements for each of the Endpoint Protection Platform Market project scopes goal statements?

185. Will the risk documents be filed?

186. Identify how your team and you will create the Endpoint Protection Platform Market project scope statement and the work breakdown structure (WBS). Document how you will create the Endpoint Protection Platform Market project scope statement

and WBS, and make sure you answer the following questions: In defining Endpoint Protection Platform Market project scope and the WBS, will you and your Endpoint Protection Platform Market project team be using methods defined by your organization, methods defined by the Endpoint Protection Platform Market project management office (PMO), or other methods?

187. Has a method and process for requirement tracking been developed?

188. Elements that deal with providing the detail?

189. Has everyone approved the Endpoint Protection Platform Market projects scope statement?

190. Will there be a Change Control Process in place?

191. Will the Endpoint Protection Platform Market project risks be managed according to the Endpoint Protection Platform Market projects risk management process?

192. Once its defined, what is the stability of the Endpoint Protection Platform Market project scope?

193. Is the Endpoint Protection Platform Market project organization documented and on file?

194. What are the possible consequences should a risk come to occur?

195. Have you been able to thoroughly document the Endpoint Protection Platform Market projects assumptions and constraints?

196. If there are vendors, have they signed off on the Endpoint Protection Platform Market project Plan?

197. Did your Endpoint Protection Platform Market project ask for this?

198. What process would you recommend for creating the Endpoint Protection Platform Market project scope statement?

2.7 Assumption and Constraint Log: Endpoint Protection Platform Market

199. Security analysis has access to information that is sanitized?

200. Are there processes defining how software will be developed including development methods, overall timeline for development, software product standards, and traceability?

201. Are there standards for code development?

202. Have all stakeholders been identified?

203. What worked well?

204. What other teams / processes would be impacted by changes to the current process, and how?

205. What strengths do you have?

206. Do the requirements meet the standards of correctness, completeness, consistency, accuracy, and readability?

207. Has a Endpoint Protection Platform Market project Communications Plan been developed?

208. How are new requirements or changes to requirements identified?

209. Have Endpoint Protection Platform Market

project management standards and procedures been established and documented?

210. Is this process still needed?

211. Is the steering committee active in Endpoint Protection Platform Market project oversight?

212. Is the process working, and people are not executing in compliance of the process?

213. Have all necessary approvals been obtained?

214. What is positive about the current process?

215. Does the system design reflect the requirements?

216. Are there processes in place to ensure that all the terms and code concepts have been documented consistently?

217. Does the Endpoint Protection Platform Market project have a formal Endpoint Protection Platform Market project Plan?

218. What does an audit system look like?

2.8 Work Breakdown Structure: Endpoint Protection Platform Market

219. Can you make it?

220. What is the probability of completing the Endpoint Protection Platform Market project in less that xx days?

221. Is the work breakdown structure (wbs) defined and is the scope of the Endpoint Protection Platform Market project clear with assigned deliverable owners?

222. Why is it useful?

223. Do you need another level?

224. How big is a work-package?

225. Is it a change in scope?

226. How will you and your Endpoint Protection Platform Market project team define the Endpoint Protection Platform Market projects scope and work breakdown structure?

227. How far down?

228. When does it have to be done?

229. Where does it take place?

230. When do you stop?

231. What is the probability that the Endpoint Protection Platform Market project duration will exceed xx weeks?

232. Who has to do it?

233. How much detail?

234. Why would you develop a Work Breakdown Structure?

235. How many levels?

2.9 WBS Dictionary: Endpoint Protection Platform Market

236. Are indirect costs accumulated for comparison with the corresponding budgets?

237. Is each control account assigned to a single organizational element directly responsible for the work and identifiable to a single element of the CWBS?

238. Are all elements of indirect expense identified to overhead cost budgets of Endpoint Protection Platform Market projections?

239. Does the contractors system provide unit costs, equivalent unit or lot costs in terms of labor, material, other direct, and indirect costs?

240. Are meaningful indicators identified for use in measuring the status of cost and schedule performance?

241. Are data elements reconcilable between internal summary reports and reports forwarded to us?

242. Changes in the direct base to which overhead costs are allocated?

243. Are the contractors estimates of costs at completion reconcilable with cost data reported to us?

244. What is the goal?

245. Does the scheduling system provide for the identification of work progress against technical and other milestones, and also provide for forecasts of completion dates of scheduled work?

246. Detailed schedules which support control account and work package start and completion dates/events?

247. Are your organizations and items of cost assigned to each pool identified?

248. Identify potential or actual overruns and underruns?

249. Are internal budgets for authorized, and not priced changes based on the contractors resource plan for accomplishing the work?

250. The already stated responsible for overhead performance control of related costs?

251. Are overhead budgets and costs being handled according to the disclosure statement when applicable, or otherwise properly classified (for example, engineering overhead, IR&D)?

252. Are indirect costs charged to the appropriate indirect pools and incurring organization?

253. The Endpoint Protection Platform Market projected business base for each period?

254. Are the requirements for all items of overhead

established by rational, traceable processes?

255. Performance to date and material commitment?

2.10 Schedule Management Plan: Endpoint Protection Platform Market

256. Are mitigation strategies identified?

257. Is there a formal set of procedures supporting Issues Management?

258. Are the schedule estimates reasonable given the Endpoint Protection Platform Market project?

259. List all schedule constraints here. Must the Endpoint Protection Platform Market project be complete by a specified date?

260. Must the Endpoint Protection Platform Market project be complete by a specified date?

261. Are Endpoint Protection Platform Market project team members committed fulltime?

262. Are there checklists created to determine if all quality processes are followed?

263. Are actuals compared against estimates to analyze and correct variances?

264. What threats might prevent you from getting there?

265. Are tasks tracked by hours?

266. What will be the format of the schedule model?

267. Are internal Endpoint Protection Platform Market project status meetings held at reasonable intervals?

268. Have the key elements of a coherent Endpoint Protection Platform Market project management strategy been established?

269. Does the Endpoint Protection Platform Market project have a Quality Culture?

270. Is a payment system in place with proper reviews and approvals?

271. How relevant is this attribute to this Endpoint Protection Platform Market project or audit?

272. Are right task and resource calendars used in the IMS?

273. Were Endpoint Protection Platform Market project team members involved in detailed estimating and scheduling?

274. Are assumptions being identified, recorded, analyzed, qualified and closed?

2.11 Activity List: Endpoint Protection Platform Market

275. How can the Endpoint Protection Platform Market project be displayed graphically to better visualize the activities?

276. How will it be performed?

277. How difficult will it be to do specific activities on this Endpoint Protection Platform Market project?

278. What is the total time required to complete the Endpoint Protection Platform Market project if no delays occur?

279. The wbs is developed as part of a joint planning session. and how do you know that youhave done this right?

280. What are the critical bottleneck activities?

281. Is infrastructure setup part of your Endpoint Protection Platform Market project?

282. How much slack is available in the Endpoint Protection Platform Market project?

283. What will be performed?

284. What is the LF and LS for each activity?

285. Can you determine the activity that must finish,

before this activity can start?

286. Where will it be performed?

287. For other activities, how much delay can be tolerated?

288. When will the work be performed?

289. How detailed should a Endpoint Protection Platform Market project get?

290. What is your organizations history in doing similar activities?

291. In what sequence?

2.12 Activity Attributes: Endpoint Protection Platform Market

292. Activity: what is In the Bag?

293. How many resources do you need to complete the work scope within a limit of X number of days?

294. Is there anything planned that does not need to be here?

295. Resources to accomplish the work?

296. Activity: what is Missing?

297. Time for overtime?

298. How else could the items be grouped?

299. What is missing?

300. Do you feel very comfortable with your prediction?

301. Where else does it apply?

302. Resource is assigned to?

303. How much activity detail is required?

304. Are the required resources available or need to be acquired?

305. Is there a trend during the year?

306. What activity do you think you should spend the most time on?

307. Have constraints been applied to the start and finish milestones for the phases?

308. How many days do you need to complete the work scope with a limit of X number of resources?

2.13 Milestone List: Endpoint Protection Platform Market

309. Reliability of data, plan predictability?

310. Do you foresee any technical risks or developmental challenges?

311. Timescales, deadlines and pressures?

312. How soon can the activity start?

313. Who will manage the Endpoint Protection Platform Market project on a day-to-day basis?

314. What is the market for your technology, product or service?

315. What are your competitors vulnerabilities?

316. Environmental effects?

317. How will the milestone be verified?

318. Sustainable financial backing?

319. Insurmountable weaknesses?

320. How late can each activity be finished and started?

321. It is to be a narrative text providing the crucial aspects of your Endpoint Protection Platform Market

project proposal answering what, who, how, when and where?

322. What has been done so far?

323. How will you get the word out to customers?

324. Loss of key staff?

325. How do you manage time?

326. Can you derive how soon can the whole Endpoint Protection Platform Market project finish?

2.14 Network Diagram: Endpoint Protection Platform Market

327. Will crashing x weeks return more in benefits than it costs?

328. What are the Key Success Factors?

329. Are you on time?

330. Planning: who, how long, what to do?

331. What are the tools?

332. What is the completion time?

333. What job or jobs follow it?

334. What activities must occur simultaneously with this activity?

335. How confident can you be in your milestone dates and the delivery date?

336. What to do and When?

337. What is the probability of completing the Endpoint Protection Platform Market project in less that xx days?

338. Exercise: what is the probability that the Endpoint Protection Platform Market project duration will exceed xx weeks?

339. Are the gantt chart and/or network diagram updated periodically and used to assess the overall Endpoint Protection Platform Market project timetable?

340. Are the required resources available?

341. What activities must follow this activity?

342. How difficult will it be to do specific activities on this Endpoint Protection Platform Market project?

343. What can be done concurrently?

344. Why must you schedule milestones, such as reviews, throughout the Endpoint Protection Platform Market project?

345. What job or jobs could run concurrently?

346. What controls the start and finish of a job?

2.15 Activity Resource Requirements: Endpoint Protection Platform Market

347. How do you handle petty cash?

348. How many signatures do you require on a check and does this match what is in your policy and procedures?

349. Organizational Applicability?

350. Why do you do that?

351. Anything else?

352. What is the Work Plan Standard?

353. Which logical relationship does the PDM use most often?

354. Other support in specific areas?

355. When does monitoring begin?

356. What are constraints that you might find during the Human Resource Planning process?

357. Do you use tools like decomposition and rolling-wave planning to produce the activity list and other outputs?

358. Are there unresolved issues that need to be addressed?

2.16 Resource Breakdown Structure: Endpoint Protection Platform Market

359. Which resource planning tool provides information on resource responsibility and accountability?

360. What defines a successful Endpoint Protection Platform Market project?

361. What is Endpoint Protection Platform Market project communication management?

362. Who will be used as a Endpoint Protection Platform Market project team member?

363. How difficult will it be to do specific activities on this Endpoint Protection Platform Market project?

364. The list could probably go on, but, the thing that you would most like to know is, How long & How much?

365. Who needs what information?

366. Which resources should be in the resource pool?

367. What defines a successful Endpoint Protection Platform Market project?

368. Why do you do it?

369. Who will use the system?

370. What is the difference between % Complete and % work?

371. Who is allowed to see what data about which resources?

372. Why time management?

373. Why is this important?

374. When do they need the information?

375. What is the primary purpose of the human resource plan?

2.17 Activity Duration Estimates: Endpoint Protection Platform Market

376. What are the three main outputs of quality control?

377. What is earned value?

378. What steps did your organization take to earn this prestigious quality award?

379. If the optimiztic estimate for an activity is 12days, and the pessimistic estimate is 18days, what is the standard deviation of this activity?

380. Sigma Endpoint Protection Platform Market project?

381. Which does one need in order to complete schedule development?

382. Endpoint Protection Platform Market project has three critical paths. Which BEST describes how this affects the Endpoint Protection Platform Market project?

383. Does a process exist to determine which risk events to accept and which events to disregard?

384. Mass, power, cost ... why not time?

385. What is the BEST thing to do?

386. How much time is required to develop it?

387. What type of activity sequencing method is required for corresponding activities?

388. Is action taken to increase the effectiveness and efficiency of Endpoint Protection Platform Market projects?

389. What are the main parts of a scope statement?

390. Why is it difficult to use Endpoint Protection Platform Market project management software well?

391. Will outside resources be needed to help in its development?

392. How does poking fun at technical professionals communications skills impact the industry and educational programs?

393. Are reward and recognition systems defined to promote or reinforce desired behavior?

394. Which includes asking team members about the time estimates for activities and reaching agreement on the calendar date for each activity?

395. Does a process exist to determine the potential loss or gain if risk events occur?

2.18 Duration Estimating Worksheet: Endpoint Protection Platform Market

396. What utility impacts are there?

397. Is a construction detail attached (to aid in explanation)?

398. Is this operation cost effective?

399. When do the individual activities need to start and finish?

400. When does your organization expect to be able to complete it?

401. Can the Endpoint Protection Platform Market project be constructed as planned?

402. Do any colleagues have experience with your organization and/or RFPs?

403. What is your role?

404. Is the Endpoint Protection Platform Market project responsive to community need?

405. Why estimate costs?

406. Done before proceeding with this activity or what can be done concurrently?

407. How can the Endpoint Protection Platform

Market project be displayed graphically to better visualize the activities?

408. What work will be included in the Endpoint Protection Platform Market project?

409. What questions do you have?

410. Value pocket identification & quantification what are value pockets?

411. Define the work as completely as possible. What work will be included in the Endpoint Protection Platform Market project?

412. What is next?

413. How should ongoing costs be monitored to try to keep the Endpoint Protection Platform Market project within budget?

2.19 Project Schedule: Endpoint Protection Platform Market

414. Did the Endpoint Protection Platform Market project come in under budget?

415. Did the final product meet or exceed user expectations?

416. Schedule/cost recovery?

417. Is the Endpoint Protection Platform Market project schedule available for all Endpoint Protection Platform Market project team members to review?

418. How can you fix it?

419. How can you minimize or control changes to Endpoint Protection Platform Market project schedules?

420. If you can not fix it, how do you do it differently?

421. Your Endpoint Protection Platform Market project management plan results in a Endpoint Protection Platform Market project schedule that is too long. If the Endpoint Protection Platform Market project network diagram cannot change and you have extra personnel resources, what is the BEST thing to do?

422. If there are any qualifying green components to this Endpoint Protection Platform Market project, what portion of the total Endpoint Protection

Platform Market project cost is green?

423. How effectively were issues able to be resolved without impacting the Endpoint Protection Platform Market project Schedule or Budget?

424. What is Endpoint Protection Platform Market project management?

425. Activity charts and bar charts are graphical representations of a Endpoint Protection Platform Market project schedule ...how do they differ?

426. Was the Endpoint Protection Platform Market project schedule reviewed by all stakeholders and formally accepted?

427. Are you working on the right risks?

428. How can slack be negative?

429. Are procedures defined by which the Endpoint Protection Platform Market project schedule may be changed?

430. What is risk?

431. Meet requirements?

2.20 Cost Management Plan: Endpoint Protection Platform Market

432. Are milestone deliverables effectively tracked and compared to Endpoint Protection Platform Market project plan?

433. Was your organizations estimating methodology being used and followed?

434. Schedule preparation – how will the schedules be prepared during each phase of the Endpoint Protection Platform Market project?

435. Are Endpoint Protection Platform Market project contact logs kept up to date?

436. Are status reports received per the Endpoint Protection Platform Market project Plan?

437. Is your organization certified as a broker of the products/supplies?

438. Technical and functional?

439. What is Endpoint Protection Platform Market project cost management?

440. Are estimating assumptions and constraints captured?

441. Are multiple estimation methods being employed?

442. What are the Endpoint Protection Platform Market project objectives?

443. Similar Endpoint Protection Platform Market projects?

444. Has a provision been made to reassess Endpoint Protection Platform Market project risks at various Endpoint Protection Platform Market project stages?

445. What weaknesses do you have?

446. Are the quality tools and methods identified in the Quality Plan appropriate to the Endpoint Protection Platform Market project?

447. Milestones – what are the key dates in executing the contract plan?

448. Are all vendor contracts closed out?

2.21 Activity Cost Estimates: Endpoint Protection Platform Market

449. How quickly can the task be done with the skills available?

450. Maintenance Reserve?

451. Would you hire them again?

452. Vac -variance at completion, how much over/ under budget do you expect to be?

453. Can you change your activities?

454. Are data needed on characteristics of care?

455. One way to define activities is to consider how organization employees describe jobs to families and friends. You basically want to know, What do you do?

456. Was the consultant knowledgeable about the program?

457. Why do you manage cost?

458. What are you looking for?

459. Were the tasks or work products prepared by the consultant useful?

460. What procedures are put in place regarding bidding and cost comparisons, if any?

461. How do you manage cost?

462. What is the last item a Endpoint Protection Platform Market project manager must do to finalize Endpoint Protection Platform Market project close-out?

463. How do you change activities?

464. Where can you get activity reports?

465. Estimated cost?

466. What happens if you cannot produce the documentation for the single audit?

467. Does the activity use a common approach or business function to deliver its results?

2.22 Cost Estimating Worksheet: Endpoint Protection Platform Market

468. Who is best positioned to know and assist in identifying corresponding factors?

469. Is the Endpoint Protection Platform Market project responsive to community need?

470. What happens to any remaining funds not used?

471. Is it feasible to establish a control group arrangement?

472. What info is needed?

473. What can be included?

474. Does the Endpoint Protection Platform Market project provide innovative ways for stakeholders to overcome obstacles or deliver better outcomes?

475. How will the results be shared and to whom?

476. Ask: are others positioned to know, are others credible, and will others cooperate?

477. Will the Endpoint Protection Platform Market project collaborate with the local community and leverage resources?

478. What additional Endpoint Protection Platform Market project(s) could be initiated as a result of this

Endpoint Protection Platform Market project?

479. Can a trend be established from historical performance data on the selected measure and are the criteria for using trend analysis or forecasting methods met?

480. What will others want?

481. Identify the timeframe necessary to monitor progress and collect data to determine how the selected measure has changed?

482. What costs are to be estimated?

483. What is the estimated labor cost today based upon this information?

484. What is the purpose of estimating?

2.23 Cost Baseline: Endpoint Protection Platform Market

485. What would the life cycle costs be?

486. What is cost and Endpoint Protection Platform Market project cost management?

487. Have all approved changes to the cost baseline been identified and impact on the Endpoint Protection Platform Market project documented?

488. Does the suggested change request seem to represent a necessary enhancement to the product?

489. Review your risk triggers -have your risks changed?

490. Where do changes come from?

491. What deliverables come first?

492. How accurate do cost estimates need to be?

493. Has operations management formally accepted responsibility for operating and maintaining the product(s) or service(s) delivered by the Endpoint Protection Platform Market project?

494. Is there anything unique in this Endpoint Protection Platform Market projects scope statement that will affect resources?

495. Has the Endpoint Protection Platform Market projected annual cost to operate and maintain the product(s) or service(s) been approved and funded?

496. Who will use corresponding metrics ?

497. Will the Endpoint Protection Platform Market project fail if the change request is not executed?

498. What is it ?

499. Have the lessons learned been filed with the Endpoint Protection Platform Market project Management Office?

500. Has training and knowledge transfer of the operations organization been completed?

501. Impact to environment?

502. Pcs for your new business. what would the life cycle costs be?

2.24 Quality Management Plan: Endpoint Protection Platform Market

503. Are qmps good forever?

504. How do you ensure that your sampling methods and procedures meet your data needs?

505. Is staff trained on the software technologies that are being used on the Endpoint Protection Platform Market project?

506. Contradictory information between document sections?

507. Are you following the quality standards?

508. Sampling part of task?

509. Who is responsible for approving the qapp?

510. How does training support what is important to your organization and the individual?

511. How does your organization use comparative data and information to improve organizational performance?

512. How do senior leaders review organizational performance?

513. How do senior leaders create an environment that encourages learning and innovation?

514. What are you trying to accomplish?

515. Are there processes in place to ensure internal consistency between the source code components?

516. What are your results for key measures/indicators of accomplishment of organizational strategy?

517. Methodology followed?

518. Who is responsible?

519. What field records are generated?

520. How does your organization maintain a safe and healthy work environment?

521. Does the program use modeling in the permitting or decision-making processes?

2.25 Quality Metrics: Endpoint Protection Platform Market

522. Are interface issues coordinated?

523. How can the effectiveness of each of the activities be measured?

524. What are your organizations expectations for its quality Endpoint Protection Platform Market project?

525. Were quality attributes reported?

526. Is quality culture a competitive advantage?

527. Where is quality now?

528. What makes a visualization memorable?

529. Are applicable standards referenced and available?

530. Were number of defects identified?

531. Does risk analysis documentation meet standards?

532. Are documents on hand to provide explanations of privacy and confidentiality?

533. Is there a set of procedures to capture, analyze and act on quality metrics?

534. What metrics do you measure?

535. What approved evidence based screening tools can be used?

536. Can visual measures help you to filter visualizations of interest?

537. How exactly do you define when differences exist?

538. Which data do others need in one place to target areas of improvement?

539. Who is willing to lead?

2.26 Process Improvement Plan: Endpoint Protection Platform Market

540. Does explicit definition of the measures exist?

541. Everyone agrees on what process improvement is, right?

542. Has the time line required to move measurement results from the points of collection to databases or users been established?

543. What lessons have you learned so far?

544. Are you making progress on the goals?

545. How do you manage quality?

546. What personnel are the champions for the initiative?

547. Does your process ensure quality?

548. Has a process guide to collect the data been developed?

549. Have storage and access mechanisms and procedures been determined?

550. To elicit goal statements, do you ask a question such as, What do you want to achieve?

551. What is quality and how will you ensure it?

552. Modeling current processes is great, and will you ever see a return on that investment?

553. Are you making progress on the improvement framework?

554. Why do you want to achieve the goal?

555. How do you measure?

556. Are you meeting the quality standards?

557. What makes people good SPI coaches?

2.27 Responsibility Assignment Matrix: Endpoint Protection Platform Market

558. What do you need to implement earned value management?

559. The total budget for the contract (including estimates for authorized and unpriced work)?

560. Wbs elements contractually specified for reporting of status (lowest level only)?

561. Authorization to proceed with all authorized work?

562. The staff interests – is the group or the person interested in working for this Endpoint Protection Platform Market project?

563. All cwbs elements specified for external reporting?

564. What cost control tool do many experts say is crucial to Endpoint Protection Platform Market project management?

565. What will the work cost?

566. Is work properly classified as measured effort, LOE, or apportioned effort and appropriately separated?

567. What can you do to improve productivity?

568. What happens when others get pulled for higher priority Endpoint Protection Platform Market projects?

569. Are detailed work packages planned as far in advance as practicable?

570. Is all contract work included in the CWBS?

571. What expertise is not available in your department?

572. Identify potential or actual budget-based and time-based schedule variances?

573. What materials and procurements needed?

574. How do you manage human resources?

575. Does each role with Accountable responsibility have the authority within your organization to make the required decisions?

576. Are the overhead pools formally and adequately identified?

577. Are management actions taken to reduce indirect costs when there are significant adverse variances?

2.28 Roles and Responsibilities: Endpoint Protection Platform Market

578. Once the responsibilities are defined for the Endpoint Protection Platform Market project, have the deliverables, roles and responsibilities been clearly communicated to every participant?

579. Have you ever been a part of this team?

580. Where are you most strong as a supervisor?

581. Key conclusions and recommendations: Are conclusions and recommendations relevant and acceptable?

582. What is working well within your organizations performance management system?

583. Does the team have access to and ability to use data analysis tools?

584. What is working well?

585. Attainable / achievable: the goal is attainable; can you actually accomplish the goal?

586. Is the data complete?

587. Do you take the time to clearly define roles and responsibilities on Endpoint Protection Platform Market project tasks?

588. What expectations were met?

589. Required skills, knowledge, experience?

590. Do the values and practices inherent in the culture of your organization foster or hinder the process?

591. Accountabilities: what are the roles and responsibilities of individual team members?

592. Are governance roles and responsibilities documented?

593. Are your policies supportive of a culture of quality data?

594. What should you highlight for improvement?

595. Be specific; avoid generalities. Thank you and great work alone are insufficient. What exactly do you appreciate and why?

596. What specific behaviors did you observe?

2.29 Human Resource Management Plan: Endpoint Protection Platform Market

597. Is a stakeholder management plan in place that covers topics?

598. Are Endpoint Protection Platform Market project team roles and responsibilities identified and documented?

599. Have the key elements of a coherent Endpoint Protection Platform Market project management strategy been established?

600. Are the key elements of a Endpoint Protection Platform Market project Charter present?

601. Are Endpoint Protection Platform Market project team members involved in detailed estimating and scheduling?

602. Are enough systems & user personnel assigned to the Endpoint Protection Platform Market project?

603. Has the Endpoint Protection Platform Market project manager been identified?

604. Is pert / critical path or equivalent methodology being used?

605. What is the boss?

606. Who needs training?

607. Does all Endpoint Protection Platform Market project documentation reside in a common repository for easy access?

608. Are Endpoint Protection Platform Market project team members committed fulltime?

609. Has the scope management document been updated and distributed to help prevent scope creep?

610. Is there an approved case?

611. Is Endpoint Protection Platform Market project work proceeding in accordance with the original Endpoint Protection Platform Market project schedule?

2.30 Communications Management Plan: Endpoint Protection Platform Market

612. What steps can you take for a positive relationship?

613. Are others needed?

614. Do you prepare stakeholder engagement plans?

615. Do you then often overlook a key stakeholder or stakeholder group?

616. What approaches to you feel are the best ones to use?

617. Who did you turn to if you had questions?

618. What to know?

619. Are stakeholders internal or external?

620. Do you have members of your team responsible for certain stakeholders?

621. What approaches do you use?

622. Which stakeholders are thought leaders, influences, or early adopters?

623. Are the stakeholders getting the information others need, are others consulted, are concerns

addressed?

624. How will the person responsible for executing the communication item be notified?

625. Who have you worked with in past, similar initiatives?

626. Who needs to know and how much?

627. What data is going to be required?

628. Who will use or be affected by the result of a Endpoint Protection Platform Market project?

629. What are the interrelationships?

630. How did the term stakeholder originate?

2.31 Risk Management Plan: Endpoint Protection Platform Market

631. What things might go wrong?

632. How is risk monitoring performed?

633. Market risk: will the new product be useful to your organization or marketable to others?

634. Are the participants able to keep up with the workload?

635. For software; are compilers and code generators available and suitable for the product to be built?

636. What are the chances the event will occur?

637. Prioritized components/features?

638. Are the software tools integrated with each other?

639. Havent software Endpoint Protection Platform Market projects been late before?

640. What are the cost, schedule and resource impacts if the risk does occur?

641. How is the audit profession changing?

642. What is the likelihood that your organization would accept responsibility for the risk?

643. How will the Endpoint Protection Platform Market project know if your organizations risk response actions were effective?

644. How are risk analvsis and prioritization performed?

645. Are Endpoint Protection Platform Market project requirements stable?

646. Monitoring -what factors can you track that will enable you to determine if the risk is becoming more or less likely?

647. Which is an input to the risk management process?

648. What can you do to minimize the impact if it does?

649. Costs associated with late delivery or a defective product?

650. Are the reports useful and easy to read?

2.32 Risk Register: Endpoint Protection Platform Market

651. What may happen or not go according to plan?

652. Are there any gaps in the evidence?

653. What is the probability and impact of the risk occurring?

654. What are you going to do to limit the Endpoint Protection Platform Market projects risk exposure due to the identified risks?

655. Recovery actions - planned actions taken once a risk has occurred to allow you to move on. What should you do after?

656. How well are risks controlled?

657. Can the likelihood and impact of failing to achieve corresponding recommendations and action plans be assessed?

658. Technology risk -is the Endpoint Protection Platform Market project technically feasible?

659. Does the evidence highlight any areas to advance opportunities or foster good relations. If yes what steps will be taken?

660. Who needs to know about this?

661. Manageability – have mitigations to the risk been identified?

662. What is a Risk?

663. Who is going to do it?

664. What are the assumptions and current status that support the assessment of the risk?

665. What further options might be available for responding to the risk?

666. Contingency actions - planned actions to reduce the immediate seriousness of the risk when it does occur. What should you do when?

667. Are your objectives at risk?

668. How are risks identified?

669. Budget and schedule: what are the estimated costs and schedules for performing risk-related activities?

670. How often will the Risk Management Plan and Risk Register be formally reviewed, and by whom?

2.33 Probability and Impact Assessment: Endpoint Protection Platform Market

671. How do risks change during a Endpoint Protection Platform Market project life cycle?

672. How is the risk management process used in practice?

673. Who will be in command to monitor and control the performance of the consortium members (consortium leader/client)?

674. Do you have a consistent repeatable process that is actually used?

675. What is the risk appetite?

676. Will new information become available during the Endpoint Protection Platform Market project?

677. Sensitivity analysis -which risks will have the most impact on the Endpoint Protection Platform Market project?

678. What should be done with non-critical risks?

679. How would you suggest monitoring for risk transition indicators?

680. Do end-users have realistic expectations?

681. What should be the level of difficulty in handling the technology?

682. Is the customer willing to participate in reviews?

683. Can you stabilize dynamic risk factors?

684. Are the risk data timely and relevant?

685. Are enough people available?

686. How completely has the customer been identified?

687. What things are likely to change?

688. How realistic is the timing of introduction?

689. Who will be responsible for a slippage?

690. Workarounds are determined during which step of risk management?

2.34 Probability and Impact Matrix: Endpoint Protection Platform Market

691. While preparing your risk responses, you identify additional risks. What should you do?

692. Is the number of people on the Endpoint Protection Platform Market project team adequate to do the job?

693. What are the current or emerging trends of culture?

694. Can it be enlarged by drawing people from other areas of your organization?

695. Is the delay in one subEndpoint Protection Platform Market project going to affect another?

696. What are the current requirements of the customer?

697. What would you do differently?

698. Are some people working on multiple Endpoint Protection Platform Market projects?

699. Will there be an increase in the political conservatism?

700. Have you ascribed a level of confidence to every critical technical objective?

701. What is the likelihood?

702. What will be the likely political environment during the life of the Endpoint Protection Platform Market project?

703. Brain storm – mind maps, what if?

704. To what extent is the chosen technology maturing?

705. What has the Endpoint Protection Platform Market project manager forgotten to do?

706. Which of the risk factors can be avoided altogether?

2.35 Risk Data Sheet: Endpoint Protection Platform Market

707. What are you weak at and therefore need to do better?

708. What are you here for (Mission)?

709. What do you know?

710. What if client refuses?

711. What will be the consequences if the risk happens?

712. What is the likelihood of it happening?

713. How reliable is the data source?

714. How can it happen?

715. What is the chance that it will happen?

716. Is the data sufficiently specified in terms of the type of failure being analyzed, and its frequency or probability?

717. What are you trying to achieve (Objectives)?

718. What will be the consequences if it happens?

719. Type of risk identified?

720. Whom do you serve (customers)?

721. What are the main opportunities available to you that you should grab while you can?

722. What actions can be taken to eliminate or remove risk?

723. What are the main threats to your existence?

724. What can happen?

725. Has the most cost-effective solution been chosen?

2.36 Procurement Management Plan: Endpoint Protection Platform Market

726. How long will it take for the purchase cost to be the same as the lease cost?

727. Are milestone deliverables effectively tracked and compared to Endpoint Protection Platform Market project plan?

728. Has a quality assurance plan been developed for the Endpoint Protection Platform Market project?

729. Does the business case include how the Endpoint Protection Platform Market project aligns with your organizations strategic goals & objectives?

730. What is a Endpoint Protection Platform Market project Management Plan?

731. Are quality metrics defined?

732. Is the steering committee active in Endpoint Protection Platform Market project oversight?

733. Are software metrics formally captured, analyzed and used as a basis for other Endpoint Protection Platform Market project estimates?

734. Have all unresolved risks been documented?

735. Have all documents been archived in a Endpoint Protection Platform Market project repository for each

release?

736. Do you have the reasons why the changes to your organizational systems and capabilities are required?

737. Are the appropriate IT resources adequate to meet planned commitments?

738. Similar Endpoint Protection Platform Market projects?

739. Have all involved Endpoint Protection Platform Market project stakeholders and work groups committed to the Endpoint Protection Platform Market project?

740. Sensitivity analysis?

741. Are the budget estimates reasonable?

742. Has your organization readiness assessment been conducted?

2.37 Source Selection Criteria: Endpoint Protection Platform Market

743. What are open book debriefings?

744. What aspects should the contracting officer brief the Endpoint Protection Platform Market project on prior to evaluation of proposals?

745. Is the contracting office likely to receive more purchase requests for this item or service during the coming year?

746. With the rapid changes in information technology, will media be readable in five or ten years?

747. Why promote competition?

748. Will the technical evaluation factor unnecessarily force the acquisition into a higher-priced market segment?

749. How will you evaluate offerors proposals?

750. Are resultant proposal revisions allowed?

751. How can solicitation Schedules be improved to yield more effective price competition?

752. What should a DRFP include?

753. Has all proposal data been loaded?

754. How will you decide an evaluators write up is sufficient?

755. How can the methods of publicizing the buy be tailored to yield more effective price competition?

756. Who is on the Source Selection Advisory Committee?

757. Are there any common areas of weaknesses or deficiencies in the proposals in the competitive range?

758. In which phase of the acquisition process cycle does source qualifications reside?

759. How do you facilitate evaluation against published criteria?

760. How should the oral presentations be handled?

761. What should be considered?

762. Is the offeror pricing what is technically proposed?

2.38 Stakeholder Management Plan: Endpoint Protection Platform Market

763. Is the communication plan being followed?

764. Are Endpoint Protection Platform Market project contact logs kept up to date?

765. Who will be collecting information?

766. Are all payments made according to the contract(s)?

767. How will the equipment be verified?

768. Are the people assigned to the Endpoint Protection Platform Market project sufficiently qualified?

769. Are risk triggers captured?

770. Are formal code reviews conducted?

771. Has the Endpoint Protection Platform Market project scope been baselined?

772. What is the drawback in using qualitative Endpoint Protection Platform Market project selection techniques?

773. Are action items captured and managed?

774. Has a Endpoint Protection Platform Market

project Communications Plan been developed?

775. Why would you develop a Endpoint Protection Platform Market project Business Plan?

776. Will the current technology alter during the life of the Endpoint Protection Platform Market project?

777. Who is accountable for the achievement of the targeted outcome(s) and reports on the progress towards the target?

778. Do all stakeholders know how to access this repository and where to find the Endpoint Protection Platform Market project documentation?

2.39 Change Management Plan: Endpoint Protection Platform Market

779. Is a training information sheet available?

780. Does this change represent a completely new process for your organization, or a different application of an existing process?

781. What risks may occur upfront?

782. What did the people around you say about it?

783. Who is the audience for change management activities?

784. Will the culture embrace or reject this change?

785. Who is the target audience of the piece of information?

786. What are the responsibilities assigned to each role?

787. How will you deal with anger about the restricting of communications due to confidentiality considerations?

788. What are the current methods of sharing information and do there need to be new ones developed?

789. What type of materials/channels will be available

to leverage?

790. Is there support for this application(s) and are the details available for distribution?

791. Are there resource implications for your communications strategy?

792. Will the readiness criteria be met prior to the training roll out?

793. When developing your communication plan do you address : When should the given message be communicated?

794. Who will fund the training?

795. Who might be able to help you the most?

796. Who will be the change levers?

797. Is there a need for new relationships to be built?

3.0 Executing Process Group: Endpoint Protection Platform Market

798. Were sponsors and decision makers available when needed outside regularly scheduled meetings?

799. Specific - is the objective clear in terms of what, how, when, and where the situation will be changed?

800. What is in place for ensuring adequate change control on Endpoint Protection Platform Market projects that involve outside contracts?

801. What are the main parts of the scope statement?

802. How well did the chosen processes produce the expected results?

803. Are escalated issues resolved promptly?

804. If action is called for, what form should it take?

805. How do you measure difficulty?

806. What is the difference between conceptual, application, and evaluative questions?

807. Do your results resemble a normal distribution?

808. When do you share the scorecard with managers?

809. How well did the chosen processes fit the needs

of the Endpoint Protection Platform Market project?

810. What business situation is being addressed?

811. It under budget or over budget?

812. How can your organization use a weighted decision matrix to evaluate proposals as part of source selection?

813. What are crucial elements of successful Endpoint Protection Platform Market project plan execution?

814. Is the program supported by national and/or local organizations?

815. How well defined and documented were the Endpoint Protection Platform Market project management processes you chose to use?

816. Do the products created live up to the necessary quality?

817. When is the appropriate time to bring the scorecard to Board meetings?

3.1 Team Member Status Report: Endpoint Protection Platform Market

818. Are the attitudes of staff regarding Endpoint Protection Platform Market project work improving?

819. What is to be done?

820. Does every department have to have a Endpoint Protection Platform Market project Manager on staff?

821. When a teams productivity and success depend on collaboration and the efficient flow of information, what generally fails them?

822. What specific interest groups do you have in place?

823. How it is to be done?

824. How much risk is involved?

825. How does this product, good, or service meet the needs of the Endpoint Protection Platform Market project and your organization as a whole?

826. Are the products of your organizations Endpoint Protection Platform Market projects meeting customers objectives?

827. How will resource planning be done?

828. Is there evidence that staff is taking a more

professional approach toward management of your organizations Endpoint Protection Platform Market projects?

829. Do you have an Enterprise Endpoint Protection Platform Market project Management Office (EPMO)?

830. Are your organizations Endpoint Protection Platform Market projects more successful over time?

831. Will the staff do training or is that done by a third party?

832. Does your organization have the means (staff, money, contract, etc.) to produce or to acquire the product, good, or service?

833. How can you make it practical?

834. The problem with Reward & Recognition Programs is that the truly deserving people all too often get left out. How can you make it practical?

835. Does the product, good, or service already exist within your organization?

836. Why is it to be done?

3.2 Change Request: Endpoint Protection Platform Market

837. How shall the implementation of changes be recorded?

838. Should staff call into the helpdesk or go to the website?

839. How do you get changes (code) out in a timely manner?

840. For which areas does this operating procedure apply?

841. What is the function of the change control committee?

842. Will new change requests be acknowledged in a timely manner?

843. How is quality being addressed on the Endpoint Protection Platform Market project?

844. How many times must the change be modified or presented to the change control board before it is approved?

845. Who can suggest changes?

846. Is it feasible to use requirements attributes as predictors of reliability?

847. Since there are no change requests in your Endpoint Protection Platform Market project at this point, what must you have before you begin?

848. What should be regulated in a change control operating instruction?

849. How can changes be graded?

850. Who needs to approve change requests?

851. Customer acceptance plan how will the customer verify the change has been implemented successfully?

852. What are the requirements for urgent changes?

853. What kind of information about the change request needs to be captured?

854. Why were your requested changes rejected or not made?

855. How is the change documented (format, content, storage)?

856. How does your organization control changes before and after software is released to a customer?

3.3 Change Log: Endpoint Protection Platform Market

857. Is the change request within Endpoint Protection Platform Market project scope?

858. Is the requested change request a result of changes in other Endpoint Protection Platform Market project(s)?

859. Is the submitted change a new change or a modification of a previously approved change?

860. When was the request approved?

861. Should a more thorough impact analysis be conducted?

862. Will the Endpoint Protection Platform Market project fail if the change request is not executed?

863. Who initiated the change request?

864. How does this change affect scope?

865. How does this relate to the standards developed for specific business processes?

866. Is the change request open, closed or pending?

867. Is the change backward compatible without limitations?

868. Do the described changes impact on the integrity or security of the system?

869. Does the suggested change request represent a desired enhancement to the products functionality?

870. When was the request submitted?

871. Is this a mandatory replacement?

872. How does this change affect the timeline of the schedule?

3.4 Decision Log: Endpoint Protection Platform Market

873. Linked to original objective?

874. At what point in time does loss become unacceptable?

875. What are the cost implications?

876. Meeting purpose; why does this team meet?

877. Is your opponent open to a non-traditional workflow, or will it likely challenge anything you do?

878. How does an increasing emphasis on cost containment influence the strategies and tactics used?

879. What makes you different or better than others companies selling the same thing?

880. Behaviors; what are guidelines that the team has identified that will assist them with getting the most out of team meetings?

881. How effective is maintaining the log at facilitating organizational learning?

882. Adversarial environment. is your opponent open to a non-traditional workflow, or will it likely challenge anything you do?

883. What was the rationale for the decision?

884. Decision-making process; how will the team make decisions?

885. Is everything working as expected?

886. Which variables make a critical difference?

887. What alternatives/risks were considered?

888. How do you define success?

889. What eDiscovery problem or issue did your organization set out to fix or make better?

890. It becomes critical to track and periodically revisit both operational effectiveness; Are you noticing all that you need to, and are you interpreting what you see effectively?

891. How consolidated and comprehensive a story can you tell by capturing currently available incident data in a central location and through a log of key decisions during an incident?

892. Do strategies and tactics aimed at less than full control reduce the costs of management or simply shift the cost burden?

3.5 Quality Audit: Endpoint Protection Platform Market

893. How does your organization know that its Mission, Vision and Values Statements are appropriate and effectively guiding your organization?

894. How does your organization know that the quality of its supervisors is appropriately effective and constructive?

895. What are your supplier audits?

896. How does your organization know that its risk management system is appropriately effective and constructive?

897. Are salvageable and salvaged medical devices stored in a manner to prevent damage and/or contamination?

898. Are the review comments incorporated?

899. How is the Strategic Plan (and other plans) reviewed and revised?

900. Health and safety arrangements; stress management workshops. How does your organization know that it provides a safe and healthy environment?

901. What is the collective experience of the team to be assigned to an audit?

902. How does your organization know that its system for recruiting the best staff possible are appropriately effective and constructive?

903. Have the risks associated with the intentions been identified, analyzed and appropriate responses developed?

904. Is your organizational structure established and each positions responsibility defined?

905. What will the Observer get to Observe?

906. Are all records associated with the reconditioning of a device maintained for a minimum of two years after the sale or disposal of the last device within a lot of merchandise?

907. How does your organization know that its system for commercializing research outputs is appropriately effective and constructive?

908. Can your organization demonstrate exactly how and why results were achieved?

909. Does your organization have set of goals, objectives, strategies and targets that are clearly understood by the Board and staff?

910. How does your organization know that it provides a safe and healthy environment?

911. How does your organization know that its relationships with industry and employers are appropriately effective and constructive?

912. Are people allowed to contribute ideas?

3.6 Team Directory: Endpoint Protection Platform Market

913. Where will the product be used and/or delivered or built when appropriate?

914. Process decisions: are all start-up, turn over and close out requirements of the contract satisfied?

915. Process decisions: do job conditions warrant additional actions to collect job information and document on-site activity?

916. Does a Endpoint Protection Platform Market project team directory list all resources assigned to the Endpoint Protection Platform Market project?

917. Who are the Team Members?

918. Decisions: what could be done better to improve the quality of the constructed product?

919. Process decisions: do invoice amounts match accepted work in place?

920. What are you going to deliver or accomplish?

921. Who should receive information (all stakeholders)?

922. Who is the Sponsor?

923. How will the team handle changes?

924. Who will write the meeting minutes and distribute?

925. Days from the time the issue is identified?

926. When will you produce deliverables?

927. How does the team resolve conflicts and ensure tasks are completed?

928. Who will report Endpoint Protection Platform Market project status to all stakeholders?

929. Process decisions: how well was task order work performed?

930. What needs to be communicated?

931. Why is the work necessary?

932. Is construction on schedule?

3.7 Team Operating Agreement: Endpoint Protection Platform Market

933. Do you post meeting notes and the recording (if used) and notify participants?

934. Are there differences in access to communication and collaboration technology based on team member location?

935. What is a Virtual Team?

936. What is group supervision?

937. Do you ask participants to close laptops and place mobile devices on silent on the table while the meeting is in progress?

938. What is the number of cases currently teamed?

939. Communication protocols: how will the team communicate?

940. Did you prepare participants for the next meeting?

941. What is teaming?

942. What are the safety issues/risks that need to be addressed and/or that the team needs to consider?

943. What went well?

944. Does your team need access to all documents and information at all times?

945. Must your team members rely on the expertise of other members to complete tasks?

946. Do you post any action items, due dates, and responsibilities on the team website?

947. Do you listen for voice tone and word choice to understand the meaning behind words?

948. Did you recap the meeting purpose, time, and expectations?

949. Do team members reside in more than two countries?

950. Methodologies: how will key team processes be implemented, such as training, research, work deliverable production, review and approval processes, knowledge management, and meeting procedures?

951. Do you determine the meeting length and time of day?

952. To whom do you deliver your services?

3.8 Team Performance Assessment: Endpoint Protection Platform Market

953. To what degree does the teams approach to its work allow for modification and improvement over time?

954. To what degree does the teams work approach provide opportunity for members to engage in open interaction?

955. To what degree does the teams work approach provide opportunity for members to engage in fact-based problem solving?

956. To what degree are the goals ambitious?

957. To what degree do the goals specify concrete team work products?

958. When a reviewer complains about method variance, what is the essence of the complaint?

959. To what degree do team members feel that the purpose of the team is important, if not exciting?

960. Delaying market entry: how long is too long?

961. To what degree are staff involved as partners in the improvement process?

962. Can familiarity breed backup?

963. What is method variance?

964. To what degree do members articulate the goals beyond the team membership?

965. To what degree does the teams purpose constitute a broader, deeper aspiration than just accomplishing short-term goals?

966. What are you doing specifically to develop the leaders around you?

967. To what degree are the relative importance and priority of the goals clear to all team members?

968. How much interpersonal friction is there in your team?

969. What makes opportunities more or less obvious?

970. To what degree does the teams work approach provide opportunity for members to engage in results-based evaluation?

971. To what degree do team members understand one anothers roles and skills?

972. To what degree can the team ensure that all members are individually and jointly accountable for the teams purpose, goals, approach, and work-products?

3.9 Team Member Performance Assessment: Endpoint Protection Platform Market

973. How will they be formed?

974. What does collaboration look like?

975. What makes them effective?

976. How should adaptive assessments be implemented?

977. What are the basic principles and objectives of performance measurement and assessment?

978. Are assessment validation activities performed?

979. What innovations (if any) are developed to realize goals?

980. Goals met?

981. What are they responsible for?

982. What evidence supports your decision-making?

983. To what degree does the teams purpose contain themes that are particularly meaningful and memorable?

984. How is the timing of assessments organized (e.g., pre/post-test, single point during training, multiple

reassessment during training)?

985. To what degree are the teams goals and objectives clear, simple, and measurable?

986. What is used as a basis for instructional decisions?

987. Why do performance reviews?

988. What qualities does a successful Team leader possess?

989. What specific plans do you have for developing effective cross-platform assessments in a blended learning environment?

990. To what degree do team members articulate the teams work approach?

991. In what areas would you like to concentrate your knowledge and resources?

3.10 Issue Log: Endpoint Protection Platform Market

992. What is the impact on the Business Case?

993. What would have to change?

994. Who is the issue assigned to?

995. Who is the stakeholder?

996. In classifying stakeholders, which approach to do so are you using?

997. What date was the issue resolved?

998. What is the stakeholders political influence?

999. What effort will a change need?

1000. Do you feel a register helps?

1001. How do you reply to this question; you am new here and managing this major program. How do you suggest you build your network?

1002. In your work, how much time is spent on stakeholder identification?

1003. Is there an important stakeholder who is actively opposed and will not receive messages?

1004. Is access to the Issue Log controlled?

1005. What are the typical contents?

1006. Are there too many who have an interest in some aspect of your work?

1007. Who reported the issue?

1008. Is the issue log kept in a safe place?

4.0 Monitoring and Controlling Process Group: Endpoint Protection Platform Market

1009. Are the necessary foundations in place to ensure the sustainability of the results of the programme?

1010. What departments are involved in its daily operation?

1011. How well defined and documented were the Endpoint Protection Platform Market project management processes you chose to use?

1012. How can you make your needs known?

1013. What is the timeline?

1014. Is it what was agreed upon?

1015. How is Agile Endpoint Protection Platform Market project Management done?

1016. What kinds of things in particular are you looking for data on?

1017. How many potential communications channels exist on the Endpoint Protection Platform Market project?

1018. What good practices or successful experiences or transferable examples have been identified?

1019. How is agile Endpoint Protection Platform Market project management done?

1020. In what way has the program come up with innovative measures for problem-solving?

1021. What communication items need improvement?

1022. When will the Endpoint Protection Platform Market project be done?

1023. Did the Endpoint Protection Platform Market project team have the right skills?

1024. Are there areas that need improvement?

1025. Where is the Risk in the Endpoint Protection Platform Market project?

4.1 Project Performance Report: Endpoint Protection Platform Market

1026. To what degree will the team adopt a concrete, clearly understood, and agreed-upon approach that will result in achievement of the teams goals?

1027. To what degree is the information network consistent with the structure of the formal organization?

1028. To what degree will new and supplemental skills be introduced as the need is recognized?

1029. To what degree does the task meet individual needs?

1030. To what degree will the approach capitalize on and enhance the skills of all team members in a manner that takes into consideration other demands on members of the team?

1031. To what degree are the skill areas critical to team performance present?

1032. To what degree is the team cognizant of small wins to be celebrated along the way?

1033. How will procurement be coordinated with other Endpoint Protection Platform Market project aspects, such as scheduling and performance reporting?

1034. What degree are the relative importance and priority of the goals clear to all team members?

1035. To what degree does the information network communicate information relevant to the task?

1036. To what degree are the members clear on what they are individually responsible for and what they are jointly responsible for?

1037. To what degree can the cognitive capacity of individuals accommodate the flow of information?

1038. To what degree can the team measure progress against specific goals?

1039. To what degree do individual skills and abilities match task demands?

1040. What is the degree to which rules govern information exchange between individuals within your organization?

1041. To what degree are the structures of the formal organization consistent with the behaviors in the informal organization?

1042. To what degree is there a sense that only the team can succeed?

4.2 Variance Analysis: Endpoint Protection Platform Market

1043. Does the contractors system provide unit or lot costs when applicable?

1044. Is data disseminated to the contractors management timely, accurate, and usable?

1045. Are there changes in the direct base to which overhead costs are allocated?

1046. Who is generally responsible for monitoring and taking action on variances?

1047. Are there quarterly budgets with quarterly performance comparisons?

1048. Is cost and schedule performance measurement done in a consistent, systematic manner?

1049. What is exceptional?

1050. How do you evaluate the impact of schedule changes, work around, et?

1051. Historical experience?

1052. What types of services and expense are shared between business segments?

1053. What is the total budget for the Endpoint Protection Platform Market project (including estimates for authorized and unpriced work)?

1054. Budget versus actual. how does the monthly budget compare to actual experience?

1055. Do the rates and prices remain constant throughout the year?

1056. What business event caused the fluctuation?

1057. Favorable or unfavorable variance?

1058. Are there knowledgeable Endpoint Protection Platform Market projections of future performance?

1059. Are overhead cost budgets established for each department which has authority to incur overhead costs?

1060. Are overhead costs budgets established on a basis consistent with the anticipated direct business base?

1061. Other relevant issues of Variance Analysis -selling price or gross margin?

4.3 Earned Value Status: Endpoint Protection Platform Market

1062. Are you hitting your Endpoint Protection Platform Market projects targets?

1063. When is it going to finish?

1064. What is the unit of forecast value?

1065. Verification is a process of ensuring that the developed system satisfies the stakeholders agreements and specifications; Are you building the product right? What do you verify?

1066. Earned value can be used in almost any Endpoint Protection Platform Market project situation and in almost any Endpoint Protection Platform Market project environment. it may be used on large Endpoint Protection Platform Market projects, medium sized Endpoint Protection Platform Market projects, tiny Endpoint Protection Platform Market projects (in cut-down form), complex and simple Endpoint Protection Platform Market projects and in any market sector. some people, of course, know all about earned value, they have used it for years - but perhaps not as effectively as they could have?

1067. Where are your problem areas?

1068. Validation is a process of ensuring that the developed system will actually achieve the stakeholders desired outcomes; Are you building the right product? What do you validate?

1069. How does this compare with other Endpoint Protection Platform Market projects?

1070. How much is it going to cost by the finish?

1071. If earned value management (EVM) is so good in determining the true status of a Endpoint Protection Platform Market project and Endpoint Protection Platform Market project its completion, why is it that hardly any one uses it in information systems related Endpoint Protection Platform Market projects?

1072. Where is evidence-based earned value in your organization reported?

4.4 Risk Audit: Endpoint Protection Platform Market

1073. To what extent should analytical procedures be utilized in the risk-assessment process?

1074. Are policies communicated to all affected?

1075. Can assurance be expanded beyond the traditional audit without undermining independence?

1076. Do industry specialists and business risk auditors enhance audit reporting accuracy?

1077. What are the costs associated with late delivery or a defective product?

1078. What are the risks that could stop you from achieving your KPIs?

1079. What are the outcomes you are looking for?

1080. What are the benefits of a Enterprise wide approach to Risk Management?

1081. Are some people working on multiple Endpoint Protection Platform Market projects?

1082. Are all financial transactions accurately recorded (receipted, banked)?

1083. Do you have position descriptions for all office bearers/staff?

1084. Are risk assessments documented?

1085. Are end-users enthusiastically committed to the Endpoint Protection Platform Market project and the system/product to be built?

1086. Does your organization have any policies or procedures to guide its decision-making (code of conduct for the board, conflict of interest policy, etc.)?

1087. Management -what contingency plans do you have if the risk becomes a reality?

1088. Do you have an emergency plan?

1089. Have all involved been advised of any obligations they have to sponsors?

1090. Have you reviewed your constitution within the last twelve months?

1091. Are you meeting your legal, regulatory and compliance requirements - if not, why not?

1092. Does your auditor understand your business?

4.5 Contractor Status Report: Endpoint Protection Platform Market

1093. What is the average response time for answering a support call?

1094. Are there contractual transfer concerns?

1095. What was the budget or estimated cost for your organizations services?

1096. What was the overall budget or estimated cost?

1097. What are the minimum and optimal bandwidth requirements for the proposed solution?

1098. How does the proposed individual meet each requirement?

1099. Describe how often regular updates are made to the proposed solution. Are corresponding regular updates included in the standard maintenance plan?

1100. Who can list a Endpoint Protection Platform Market project as organization experience, your organization or a previous employee of your organization?

1101. If applicable; describe your standard schedule for new software version releases. Are new software version releases included in the standard maintenance plan?

1102. What was the final actual cost?

1103. How is risk transferred?

1104. How long have you been using the services?

1105. What process manages the contracts?

1106. What was the actual budget or estimated cost for your organizations services?

4.6 Formal Acceptance: Endpoint Protection Platform Market

1107. Have all comments been addressed?

1108. Do you buy pre-configured systems or build your own configuration?

1109. Was the sponsor/customer satisfied?

1110. What lessons were learned about your Endpoint Protection Platform Market project management methodology?

1111. Does it do what client said it would?

1112. What features, practices, and processes proved to be strengths or weaknesses?

1113. Who supplies data?

1114. What function(s) does it fill or meet?

1115. How does your team plan to obtain formal acceptance on your Endpoint Protection Platform Market project?

1116. General estimate of the costs and times to complete the Endpoint Protection Platform Market project?

1117. Did the Endpoint Protection Platform Market project achieve its MOV?

1118. Do you perform formal acceptance or burn-in tests?

1119. What is the Acceptance Management Process?

1120. Was the Endpoint Protection Platform Market project goal achieved?

1121. Was the client satisfied with the Endpoint Protection Platform Market project results?

1122. Was the Endpoint Protection Platform Market project managed well?

1123. Does it do what Endpoint Protection Platform Market project team said it would?

1124. What are the requirements against which to test, Who will execute?

1125. Was business value realized?

1126. Did the Endpoint Protection Platform Market project manager and team act in a professional and ethical manner?

5.0 Closing Process Group: Endpoint Protection Platform Market

1127. What areas does the group agree are the biggest success on the Endpoint Protection Platform Market project?

1128. Was the schedule met?

1129. How well did the team follow the chosen processes?

1130. Is the Endpoint Protection Platform Market project funded?

1131. Is this an updated Endpoint Protection Platform Market project Proposal Document?

1132. Does the close educate others to improve performance?

1133. What could have been improved?

1134. How well did the chosen processes fit the needs of the Endpoint Protection Platform Market project?

1135. What is the amount of funding and what Endpoint Protection Platform Market project phases are funded?

1136. How critical is the Endpoint Protection Platform Market project success to the success of your organization?

1137. What is the Endpoint Protection Platform Market project name and date of completion?

1138. Based on your Endpoint Protection Platform Market project communication management plan, what worked well?

1139. What is the overall risk of the Endpoint Protection Platform Market project to your organization?

1140. What was learned?

1141. Are there funding or time constraints?

5.1 Procurement Audit: Endpoint Protection Platform Market

1142. When tenders were actually rejected because they were abnormally low, were reasons for this decision given and were they sufficiently grounded?

1143. Are order quantities, deliveries and payment levels under the contract monitored by an appropriate official?

1144. Does the strategy discus the best manner of purchase, considering the types of goods and services needed?

1145. Are blank purchase order forms protected?

1146. Are receiving reports on file for all claims for equipment, supplies and materials in the paid claims file?

1147. Are all purchase orders cancelled after payment to avoid duplicate payment of the same invoice?

1148. Was a formal review of tenders received undertaken?

1149. Are there systems for recording and managing stocks (where part of contract)?

1150. Do established procedures ensure that computer programs will not pay the same group of invoices twice?

1151. When competitive dialogue was used, did the contracting authority provide sufficient justification for the use of this procedure and was the contract actually particularly complex?

1152. Is there an effective risk management system continuously monitoring procurement risk?

1153. Does the department have a procurement strategy and is it implemented?

1154. Has the award included no items different from the already stated contained in bid specifications?

1155. Did the conditions included in the contract protect the risk of non-performance by the supplier and were there no conflicting provisions?

1156. Did the conditions of contract comply with the detail provided in the procurement documents and with the outcome of the procurement procedure followed?

1157. Was the estimated contract value in line with the final cost of the contract awarded?

1158. Were standards, certifications and evidence required admissible?

1159. Are all initial purchase contracts made by the purchasing organization?

1160. Which are necessary components of a financial audit report under the Single Audit Act?

1161. Are bank accounts reconciled by an individual independent of the disbursement responsibilities?

5.2 Contract Close-Out: Endpoint Protection Platform Market

1162. How does it work?

1163. Why Outsource?

1164. Has each contract been audited to verify acceptance and delivery?

1165. How is the contracting office notified of the automatic contract close-out?

1166. Change in attitude or behavior?

1167. How/when used ?

1168. What happens to the recipient of services?

1169. Change in knowledge?

1170. Was the contract sufficiently clear so as not to result in numerous disputes and misunderstandings?

1171. Was the contract complete without requiring numerous changes and revisions?

1172. Have all acceptance criteria been met prior to final payment to contractors?

1173. What is capture management?

1174. Parties: who is involved?

1175. Have all contracts been closed?

1176. Change in circumstances?

1177. Have all contract records been included in the Endpoint Protection Platform Market project archives?

1178. Parties: Authorized?

1179. Have all contracts been completed?

1180. Was the contract type appropriate?

1181. Are the signers the authorized officials?

5.3 Project or Phase Close-Out: Endpoint Protection Platform Market

1182. Does the lesson describe a function that would be done differently the next time?

1183. Does the lesson educate others to improve performance?

1184. Were messages directly related to the release strategy or phases of the Endpoint Protection Platform Market project?

1185. Have business partners been involved extensively, and what data was required for them?

1186. What can you do better next time, and what specific actions can you take to improve?

1187. What were the goals and objectives of the communications strategy for the Endpoint Protection Platform Market project?

1188. What are they?

1189. What is this stakeholder expecting?

1190. What could be done to improve the process?

1191. Is the lesson based on actual Endpoint Protection Platform Market project experience rather than on independent research?

1192. In preparing the Lessons Learned report, should it reflect a consensus viewpoint, or should the report reflect the different individual viewpoints?

1193. Which changes might a stakeholder be required to make as a result of the Endpoint Protection Platform Market project?

1194. Planned completion date?

1195. What are the mandatory communication needs for each stakeholder?

1196. What were the actual outcomes?

1197. Were cost budgets met?

1198. If you were the Endpoint Protection Platform Market project sponsor, how would you determine which Endpoint Protection Platform Market project team(s) and/or individuals deserve recognition?

5.4 Lessons Learned: Endpoint Protection Platform Market

1199. What is the value of the deliverable?

1200. What is your organizational ideology?

1201. What regulatory constraints impact the case?

1202. What is your working hypothesis, if you have one?

1203. How efficient were Endpoint Protection Platform Market project team meetings conducted?

1204. What report generation capability is needed?

1205. How was the political and social history changed over the life of the Endpoint Protection Platform Market project?

1206. Are lessons learned documented?

1207. Did the team work well together?

1208. Recommendation: what do you recommend should be done to ensure that others throughout your organization can benefit from what you have learned?

1209. What is the frequency of group communications?

1210. Where could you improve?

1211. How effective was Endpoint Protection Platform Market project Team member training?

1212. Was the user/client satisfied with the end product?

1213. What was the methodology behind successful learning experiences, and how might they be applied to the broader challenge of your organizations knowledge management?

1214. What mistakes did you successfully avoid making?

1215. Why do you need to measure?

1216. Were any strategies or activities unsuccessful?

1217. Were the aims and objectives achieved?

1218. How well were your expectations met regarding the extent of your involvement in the Endpoint Protection Platform Market project (effort, time commitments, etc.)?

Index

address   22, 83, 139, 220
addressed   172, 202, 222, 225, 236, 256
addressing   36, 121
adequate   29, 152, 209, 214, 221
adequately   39, 196
adjust 95-96
adjusted   97
admissible   261
adopted   140
adopters   201
advance   196, 205
advantage   71, 107, 191
advantages   126, 138-139
adverse   196
advised   253
Advisory   216
affect 67, 73, 107, 109, 141, 144, 150, 187, 209, 227-228
affected   136, 138, 144-145, 202, 252
affecting   12, 17, 63
affects 175
affordable   81
against31, 104, 160, 162, 216, 247, 257
agenda   134
agendas   123
aggregate   49
agreed   145, 244
agreement   6, 107, 145, 176, 236
agreements   68, 80, 250
agrees 108, 193
aiming 112
alerts   104
aligned   22
alignment   141
aligns 213
alleged   1
alliance   79
allocate   123
allocated   51, 55, 122, 159, 248
allowed   129, 174, 215, 233
allows 10
almost 250
already   113, 160, 224, 261
altogether   210

always 10
ambitious   238
amount   19, 258
amounts   234
amplify65
analvsis   204
analysis   3, 7, 10-11, 61-62, 64, 69, 71-72, 78, 83, 88, 138,
147, 155, 186, 191, 197, 207, 214, 227, 248-249
analytical   252
analyze   2, 59, 64, 72, 162, 191
analyzed   104, 133, 163, 211, 213, 232
annual 188
another   157, 209
anothers   239
answer 11-12, 16, 28, 44, 59, 76, 93, 106, 153
answered   27, 43, 58, 75, 91, 105, 131
answering   11, 169, 254
anticipate   152
anyone   38, 121, 125
anything   166, 172, 187, 229
appear   1
appetite   207
applicable   12, 101, 148, 160, 191, 248, 254
applied   83, 101, 141, 167, 268
appointed   35, 37
appreciate   198
approach   79, 87, 126, 144, 184, 224, 238-239, 241-242, 246,
252
approaches   89-90, 201
approval   125, 237
approvals   147, 156, 163
approve   226
approved   35, 70, 133, 147, 150, 153, 187-188, 192, 200, 225,
227
approving   150, 189
Architects   8
archived   213
archives   264
around106, 130, 219, 239, 248
arriving145
articulate   239, 241
ascribed   209
asking 1, 8, 176

aspect 243
aspects   168, 215, 246
aspiration   239
assess 17, 30, 81, 105, 116, 171
assessed   89, 205
assessing   90, 96
Assessment   5-6, 9-10, 21, 141, 147, 206-207, 214, 238, 240
assets 51
assign 16
assigned   37, 135, 157, 159-160, 166, 199, 217, 219, 231,
234, 242
Assignment   5, 195
assist   9, 70, 90, 103, 185, 229
assistant   8
associated   204, 232, 252
Assumption   3, 155
assurance   20, 144, 213, 252
attached   177
attainable   33, 197
attempted   38
attempting   98
attend 24
attendance   35
attendant   80
attended   35
attention   12, 111
attitude   263
attitudes   223
attribute   163
attributes   4, 112, 148, 166, 191, 225
audience   219
audited   263
auditing   25, 93, 108
auditor 253
auditors   252
audits 231
author 1
authority   73, 196, 249, 261
authorized   142, 160, 195, 249, 264
automatic   263
available   20, 27, 36, 39, 45, 60, 65, 81, 103, 115, 164, 166,
171, 179, 183, 191, 196, 203, 206-208, 212, 219-221, 230
Average   12, 27, 43, 58, 75, 91, 105, 131, 254

colleague   129
colleagues   121, 125, 177
collect 59, 98, 186, 193, 234
collected   33, 39, 62, 66-67
collecting   217
collection   64, 193
collective   231
combine   90
coming   69, 215
command   102, 207
comments   231, 256
commitment   93, 126, 161
committed   73, 162, 200, 214, 253
committee   156, 213, 216, 225
common   184, 200, 216
community   177, 185
companies   1, 95, 229
company   8, 48, 71, 111-112, 121, 123, 129
comparable   142
compare   64, 89, 249, 251
compared   114, 162, 181, 213
comparing   89, 142
comparison   11, 159
compatible   227
compelling   34
competing   54
compilers   203
complains   238
complaint   238
complete   1, 9, 11, 32, 37, 40, 144, 162, 164, 166-167, 174-175, 177, 197, 237, 256, 263
completed   12, 28-29, 34, 38, 188, 235, 264
completely   119, 178, 208, 219
completing   107, 157, 170
completion   31-32, 133, 159-160, 170, 183, 251, 259, 266
complex   8, 110, 250, 261
complexity   17, 67
compliance   24, 47-48, 51, 69, 80, 156, 253
comply   261
components   144, 179, 190, 203, 261
compute   12
computer   260
computing   119

eDiscovery   230
edition 9
editorial   1
educate   258, 265
education   24, 101
effective   18, 26, 109, 113, 177, 204, 215-216, 229, 231-232, 240-241, 261, 268
effects 52, 168
efficiency   66, 98, 176
efficient   47, 140, 223, 267
effort   41, 46, 48, 51, 108, 142, 144, 146, 195, 242, 268
efforts   38, 83, 136
electronic   1
element   159
elements   10, 36, 72, 100, 109, 153, 159, 163, 195, 199, 222
elicit   193
eliminate   212
embarking   34
embrace   219
emergency   253
emerging   61, 99, 209
emphasis   229
employed   181
employee   88, 254
employees   17-18, 72, 121, 125, 128, 183
employers   137, 232
empower   8
enable 60, 204
enablers   129
encourage   77, 102
encourages   189
Endpoint   1-14, 16-18, 20-27, 29-51, 53-91, 93-105, 107-142, 144-148, 150, 152-160, 162-166, 168-173, 175-189, 191, 193, 195-197, 199-205, 207, 209-211, 213-215, 217-219, 221-227, 229, 231, 234-236, 238, 240, 242, 244-246, 248-254, 256-260, 263-268
end-users   207, 253
engage   114, 238-239
engagement   56, 137, 201
enhance   102, 246, 252
enhanced   123
enhancing   94
enlarged   209
enough   8, 70, 111, 116, 120, 149-150, 199, 208

ensure 31, 37, 62, 80, 109-110, 112, 123, 129, 156, 189-190, 193, 235, 239, 244, 260, 267
ensures 110
ensuring 10, 122, 221, 250
entail 51
Enterprise 224, 252
entities 51, 142
entity 1
equipment 23, 25, 217, 260
equipped 36
equitably 32
equivalent 159, 199
errors 117
escalated 221
essence 238
essential 77
essentials 126
establish 76, 95, 185
estimate 55, 57, 142, 175, 177, 256
estimated 31-32, 45, 57, 184, 186, 206, 254-255, 261
estimates 4, 36, 46, 68, 142, 159, 162, 175-176, 183, 187, 195, 213-214, 249
estimating 4, 163, 177, 181, 185-186, 199
estimation 90, 140, 145, 181
etcetera 126
ethical 21, 257
evaluate 77, 88, 91, 215, 222, 248
evaluated 134
evaluating 82, 90
evaluation 69, 81, 100, 215-216, 239
evaluative 221
evaluators 216
events 24, 84-85, 89, 160, 175-176
everyday 72
everyone 32, 40, 153, 193
everything 44, 230
evidence 11, 54, 192, 205, 223, 240, 261
evolution 44
evolve 97
exactly 192, 198, 232
examined 41
example 2, 9, 13, 23, 72, 103, 143, 160
examples 8-9, 244

293

process　　　　1-3, 5-8, 10, 28-31, 34, 40, 55, 60-73, 83, 89, 94-95, 99-101, 103-104, 133, 140, 146, 148, 150, 153-156, 172, 175-176, 193, 198, 204, 207, 216, 219, 221, 230, 234-235, 238, 244, 250, 252, 255, 257-258, 265
processes　　　51, 57, 59-63, 65-66, 69, 71, 73-74, 96, 100, 103, 134, 138, 140, 155-156, 161-162, 190, 194, 221-222, 227, 237, 244, 256, 258
produce　　　73, 172, 184, 221, 224, 235
produced　　　67, 80
producing　　　150
product　　　　1, 57, 61, 64, 121, 126, 147, 155, 168, 179, 187-188, 203-204, 223-224, 234, 250-253, 268
production　　　29, 87, 124, 237
products　　　1, 22-23, 56, 110, 117, 135, 150, 181, 183, 222-223, 228, 238
profession　　　203
program　　　17, 51, 60, 96, 134, 140-142, 183, 190, 222, 242, 245
programme　　　244
programs　　　142, 176, 224, 260
progress　　　37, 88, 98, 121, 128, 145, 160, 186, 193-194, 218, 236, 247
project 2-4, 7-9, 16-17, 38, 45, 70, 74, 96, 103, 109-111, 114-115, 118, 124-125, 127, 132-142, 144-148, 150, 152-158, 162-165, 168-171, 173, 175-182, 184-189, 191, 195, 197, 199-200, 202, 204-205, 207, 209-210, 213-215, 217-218, 222-227, 234-235, 244-246, 248, 250-251, 253-254, 256-259, 264-268
projected　　　160, 188
projects　　　　2, 52, 124, 129, 132, 134, 142, 150, 153, 157, 176, 182, 187, 196, 203, 205, 209, 214, 221, 223-224, 250-252
promising　　　126
promote　　　56, 73, 176, 215
promptly　　　221
proofing　　　83
proper 95, 163
properly　　　31, 40, 160, 195
proposal　　　169, 215, 258
proposals　　　102, 215-216, 222
proposed　　　19, 45, 82, 86, 138, 142, 146, 148, 216, 254
protect　　　72, 123, 142, 261
protected　　　66, 260

rework 45, 49
rights   1
robustness   139
routine 97
safety 110, 142, 231, 236
salvaged   231
Sampling   189
sanitized   155
satisfied   116, 234, 256-257, 268
satisfies 250
satisfying   114
savings 36, 47, 52, 68
scalable   85
scenario   41, 43
schedule   3-4, 36, 44, 95, 116, 144, 159, 162, 171, 175, 179-
181, 196, 200, 203, 206, 228, 235, 248, 254, 258
scheduled   146, 160, 221
schedules   160, 179, 181, 206, 215
scheduling   145, 160, 163, 199, 246
scheme   102
science   68
scopes 152
Scorecard   2, 12-14, 221-222
scorecards   96
Scores 14
scoring 10
screening   142, 192
seamless   113
second   12
section 12, 27, 43, 58, 75, 91, 105, 131
sections   189
sector 250
securing   56, 123
security   25, 68, 94, 105, 137, 155, 228
segment   215
segmented   39
segments   42, 109, 248
select 69, 98
selected   88, 142, 186
selecting   67, 108, 142
Selection   5, 215-217, 222
sellers   1
selling 119, 229

trying   8, 111, 125, 190, 211
twelve 253
typical 243
ubiquitous   119
ultimate   109
unclear   32
underlying   83
undermine   125
underruns   160
understand   39, 60, 133, 237, 239, 253
understood   85, 87, 122, 232, 246
undertake   65
undertaken   260
underway   82
uninformed   119
unique 113, 187
Unless 8
unpriced   195, 249
unresolved   172, 213
updated   9-10, 64, 144, 171, 200, 258
updates   10, 96, 254
upfront219
up-sell 118
urgent 226
usability   81, 116
usable 248
useful   78, 94, 157, 183, 203-204
usefully 10, 19
utility   177
utilized 252
utilizing 80
validate   48, 251
validated   28, 31, 34, 65, 73
Validation   240, 250
Validity 148
valuable   8
values 93, 126, 198, 231
variables   67, 95, 230
Variance   7, 238-239, 248-249
-variance   183
variances   145, 162, 196, 248
variation   16, 37, 62, 66, 99
various 182

CPSIA information can be obtained
at www.ICGtesting.com
Printed in the USA
BVHW040241210819
556236BV00028B/635/P